THE
OTHER
SIDE

"THE OTHER SIDE"

by Staughton Lynd

and Thomas Hayden

THE NEW AMERICAN LIBRARY

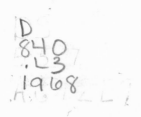

First Printing

Library of Congress Catalog Card Number: 67–15194

Published by The New American Library, Inc.
1301 Avenue of the Americas, New York,
New York 10019
Published simultaneously in Canada
by General Publishing Company, Ltd.

Printed in the United States of America

The Church of the Spirit is always
being built. It possesses no other kind
of power and authority than the power
and authority of personal lives, formed
into a community. . . .

Life is mightier than the book that
reports it. The most important thing
in the world is that our faith becomes
living experience and deed of life.

*Lines written by Norman Morrison, an American
Quaker, shortly before he burned himself
to death at the Pentagon in November, 1965*

There were those who pursued glory
Who dreamt of conquest and power,
Why evoke the days of epic battles
When subsequent misfortunes brought great sorrow?

There were those who wielded great power
Whose red-ink characters decided men's fates,
Who were fountains of knowledge and experience,
But prosperity and power engender hatred.

There were those at the head of proud armies
Who sacked palaces and overturned thrones.
In a display of might like storm and thunder,
Thousands were killed for the glory of one man.

There were those victims of injustice,
Year after year they languished in jail.
Dead, they were buried somewhere near the prison wall.
For their shroud, only a tattered rush mat.
Will their innocence ever be revealed?

There were the babies born in an inauspicious hour
Who lived only a few moments.
There's nobody now to carry them in her arms,
And heart-rending are their feeble cries.

Nguyen Du (classical Vietnamese poet),
"*Calling the Wandering Souls*," trans. *Le Hieu and
reprinted from* Vietnamese Studies, *No. 4, 1965*

CONTENTS

THE
OTHER
SIDE

1

WHY WE WENT

I

We made a Christmas journey to North Vietnam, that remote country which the American Government blames for the spreading war in Asia, and to which American citizens are forbidden to travel. This book is a diary of our trip, and a reflection on the war.

Many other private citizens had gone to North Vietnam in 1965 in the hope of doing something to stop the escalation of the war. Among them were Fenner Brockway; William Warbey, a Labor member of Parliament; British newsman James Cameron; the reporter Felix Greene; an Italian professor, Giorgio La Pira. But, so far as we know, we were the only Western citizens in Hanoi in the midst of the greatest "peace offensive" since the beginning of the war.

We went because it seemed unendurable to stand by and do nothing. Like most other Americans, we had been slow to become sensitive to what our Government was doing in this small country eight thousand miles away. That we became in some degree sensitive, and that we went, grew from our participation in the American civil rights movement; and we would like to explain how this happened.

In 1945–46, when the defeated Japanese surrendered Vietnam, when France sought to recover its former colony and what the Vietnamese call the "Resistance War" began, one of us (Staughton) was just entering college, the other (Tom) starting elementary school. That war ended in the spring of 1954 with the French defeat at the battle of Dienbienphu. Staughton was in the United States Army at the time, and remembers reading that Secretary of State John Foster Dulles, Vice-President Richard Nixon and others were urging American air strikes in support of the French. He also remembers wondering if he would be sent to Vietnam. But May, 1954, the month of Dienbienphu, was also the month of the Supreme Court decision in *Brown v. Board of Education* which set the stage for the American civil rights movement. We were little conscious of the subsequent Geneva Agreements, which banned foreign troops and foreign military bases from Vietnam, and divided the country along the 17th parallel pending a nation-wide election stipulated for 1956, but never held.

The next turning-point in Vietnamese history came in 1959–60, when sporadic opposition to the oppressive South Vietnamese Government of Ngo Dinh Diem fused into a Resistance movement (the National Liberation Front, or in derogatory American parlance, "Vietcong") patterned on the earlier Vietminh, and the Communist Government of North Vietnam (officially, the Democratic Republic of Vietnam) threw its full support behind the Southern movement.[1] Both of us

---

[1] It must be clear to the reader that we believe the present conflict originated not primarily as "aggression from the North" or as "North Vietnam's effort to conquer South Vietnam" (the titles of the two

were then preoccupied with finding ways to join the civil rights movement in the American South. Sit-ins (1960), freedom rides and the beginning of voter registration in the Southern Black Belt (1961) filled our minds. Tom did civil rights work in Georgia and Mississippi, and Staughton began a three-year teaching stint at a Negro women's college in Atlanta.

In the years that followed, Tom helped to found the Students for a Democratic Society (SDS) and then, after leaving graduate school, began to do community organization work in a Negro ghetto in Newark, New Jersey. Staughton directed the Freedom Schools of the 1964 Mississippi Summer Project and then became an assistant professor of history at Yale. The war in Vietnam intruded itself more and more insistently. At the funeral for Michael Schwerner, Andrew Goodman, and James Chaney, murdered on the first day of the 1964 Summer Project, Robert (Moses) Parris, the Project coordinator, called attention to the fact that on the day in early August when their bodies were discovered the President of the United States ordered the first bombing of North Vietnam. The lesson of all these deaths, Parris said, was that men simply had to stop killing.

This decision to escalate the war was followed in August by

United States White Papers on this subject), but rather as an essentially civil war caused by the hated dictatorship of Ngo Dinh Diem. See Philippe Devillers, "Ngo Dinh Diem and the Struggle for Reunification in Vietnam," *Vietnam: History, Documents, and Opinions on a Major World Crisis*, ed. Marvin E. Gettleman (New York, 1965), pp. 210–235; Jean Lacouture, *Vietnam: Between Two Truces* (New York, 1966), pp. 28–31, 50–56; Wilfred G. Burchett, *Vietnam: Inside Story of the Guerilla War* (New York, 1965), Chapter 8, "How Did The War Start?"

Throughout this book, "N.L.F." refers to the National Liberation Front (or Vietcong), "D.R.V." to the Democratic Republic of Vietnam (or North Vietnamese Government).

the Administration's snub of the Mississippi Freedom Democratic Party's bid for representation at the Democratic convention.

Until then Tom had hoped that a crisis of civil rights and poverty in America might compel a turning away from the Cold War. Looking back, that possibility seems to have collapsed with the decisions to bomb the North Vietnamese while barring the Freedom Democrats. From that point on, the war for freedom in Vietnam—while freedom is lacking at home— has become America's primary concern. It has served to strengthen America's reluctance to accept change and revolution anywhere in the world. Opposing the war thus became for Tom part of an opposition to racial and class prejudice in America itself.

What was one to do? At the first mass protest against the war, organized by SDS in April, 1965, Staughton spoke of how easily Americans reproach the people of Germany for failing to act against Hitler in the nineteen-thirties, and asked: what exactly did we expect them to do? He also referred to the statement made by Thoreau during the Mexican War: it is in jail "that the fugitive slave, and the Mexican prisoner on parole, and the Indian come to plead the wrongs of his race, should find" the honorable American. As a Quaker and a pacifist it was natural for Staughton to take certain personal steps: to refuse to pay taxes on his income over and above what was withheld by Yale, to encourage refusal to serve in the Army by those who could conscientiously do so. In August, 1965, Staughton, Robert Parris, and three hundred others were arrested in Washington when they attempted to "declare peace with the people of Vietnam" on the steps of the Capitol, as a means of rebuking the Congress for its failure to exercise its constitutional responsibility over war and peace. Such actions, together with the teach-ins of spring, 1965, and the first International Days of Protest on October 15 and 16, helped to stimulate questioning of the war in more conventional forms.

Yet it was all clearly not enough. The war continued to escalate. Evidence mounted that, despite Presidential assurances to the contrary, the United States had several times rebuffed diplomatic overtures from the other side. As autumn drew toward Christmas, bombing of Hanoi and Haiphong, hitherto spared by American planes, seemed imminent, and an anguished world began to cry out, in the words of an advertisement placed in the *New York Times* by many hundreds of clergymen: In the name of God, stop it! On election day, in November, Staughton's friend Norman Morrison burned himself to death at the Pentagon after reading of the bombing of children in an unprotected South Vietnamese village.

Then came the opportunity to go to North Vietnam.

Dr. Herbert Aptheker, an American historian and a leading theoretician of the American Communist Party, returned from a peace conference at Helsinki, Finland, where North Vietnamese had invited him to travel to their country with two non-Communist Americans. Herbert invited Staughton: the two knew each other and had occasionally discussed problems in American history. Staughton and Tom had met in Atlanta during the inception of the Student Nonviolent Coordinating Committee. It was arranged finally that Tom should be the third traveler.

We both worried about the effects that the trip might have on the American protest movement, and on the two of us. Internationally, we were concerned about the danger of causing a news sensation rather than achieving understanding with the North Vietnamese. Fresh in our minds were the details of the confusing and perhaps damaging episode during which the Italian professor Giorgio La Pira brought an apparent "peace feeler" from Hanoi only to have it lost in the cross fire of subsequent Washington and Hanoi commentary. We did not want to return from the other side and be criticized as inaccurate, nor did we want Washington to make the "right-to-travel" or "amateur diplomacy" issues more newsworthy than our actual findings.

With respect to the protest movement at home, we feared that organizations or other individuals might be attacked or somehow suffer from the national response to our trip. Staughton feared this because he has been singled out as a "peace leader" or "leader of the New Left" by the press. Tom feared mudslinging or other retribution against the poor people's community project for which he works. There also was a problem in Tom's case of the effect on Students for a Democratic Society, which had organized demonstrations against the war but had not taken any action which might be considered illegal.

But we felt that it was important to test whether or not persons working on domestic issues such as civil rights or poverty could also begin to take strong stands on international questions without losing their legitimacy at home. We feared that the civil rights and anti-poverty movements would be channeled into a quest for token domestic improvement with their leaders accepting American foreign policy as the price; thus tending to create an acquisitive, all-powerful America whose poor are not only narrow nationalists but wealthy in comparison with the world's people.

Then there was the question of going with a Communist. Each of us had identified strongly with those in the civil rights and peace movements who advocate a policy of "non-exclusion" toward Communists if the latter are prepared to cooperate on specific tasks with candor and without proselytizing. Going to Vietnam was a specific task which we thought someone ought to do and which we could not sidestep. We did not know if there were other ways Americans might visit Hanoi. We did know several other persons in the peace movement who had unsuccessfully sought invitations. To exhaust every alternative would mean losing precious time. Further, Staughton knew and personally trusted Herbert. We thought it would be indefensible to advocate the possibility of working with Communists domestically and a conciliatory policy toward Communists in Vietnam, yet to decline the invitation to go to Hanoi for this reason.

II

Although fact-finding about "the other side's" negotiating positions for ending the war was our principal purpose, an important by-product of the trip was the chance to confront those whom the United States Government has proclaimed its enemies in the Cold War. During World War II Edgar Snow could write a book about the Communists of Russia and China as "people on our side." As of Christmas, 1965, those same people had unequivocally become "the other side," at least so far as the American Government was concerned.

Perhaps the most stubbornly visible representatives of "the other side" today are the North Vietnamese and the National Liberation Front of South Vietnam. The United States has regarded these Vietnamese as "the other side" ever since the August, 1945, revolution which brought Ho Chi Minh and the Communist-led, but broad-based, Vietminh Front to power. Since Ho Chi Minh was a Communist himself, since he had been educated among Western Communists, his new Government was seen as an extension of what American officials called "Soviet imperialism." It did not matter that the Vietminh made their revolution with little aid from Russia and even with some aid, during World War II, from the United States Office of Strategic Services. It did not matter that the 1945 Vietnamese Declaration of Independence invoked both the French and American revolutions, and began with the words, "All men are created equal." The revolution, said American policy-makers, was Red: therefore, not popular, not genuine.

Our country's thinking about Vietnam's "other side" is conditioned also by stereotyped American attitudes toward Asians. Members of the other side are pictured by Government propaganda as interchangeable aggressors, statistics in a weekly body count, and in the words of John Mecklin of the United States Information Service, "faceless unknowns." Unofficial stereotypes fill out the image of the enemy as men whose very physical makeup is different: un-persons who can live for a week on a few balls of rice, who do not feel torture or fear death like proper Caucasians. Lyndon Johnson himself, while a congressman in 1948, warned the country against the possibility of being blackmailed by "any yellow dwarf with a pocket knife."[2]

It was easy for us to empathize with non-Communist neutralist Vietnamese, such as the students and Buddhists who demonstrated in the spring of 1966, after our return. They were asking for Freedom Now, the demand of the American civil rights movement. The press reported that "some impatient members of the Buddhist movement shouted into a public address system at the Buddhist student headquarters courtyard, 'The time for talking is past . . . Now is the time for action.'" (How often has this been said by young American

---

[2] *Congressional Record*, March 15, 1948, 80th Congress, Second Session, vol. 94, part 2, p. 2883.

rebels?) At the Marine base in Da Nang, where in September, 1965, three leaders of a similar demonstration had been tied to posts on a soccer field and shot, our Vietnamese counterparts had the courage to go out on the streets with banners saying, "Down With Ky," and "Throw Out The Generals." A leaflet handed out in Natrang by (as in Birmingham) high school students said: "Every day the future of the country becomes darker. The reputation of the nation has almost disappeared." (Wasn't that what we felt with shame and anguish about our own country?) The leaflet went on to say that generals must be made to understand that their proper role is not as leaders but as technicians. (Isn't that what we are trying to say to our generals, too?) In Hue, one banner said, "Down with the American Plot to Prevent the Summoning of a Constitutional Convention." (Hasn't this war, imposed by the President and the generals without a clear congressional mandate, caused a constitutional crisis in the United States?)

These students were not Communists, although if they came to power they would doubtless negotiate with the National Liberation Front. They were not demanding socialism, only (to use the American protest slogan) to Let the people decide. We felt they were like us, that their cause was ours as well.

Yet we also discovered that we felt empathy for those more fully "other" members of the other side, spokesmen for the Communist world in Prague and Moscow, Peking and Hanoi. After all, we call ourselves in some sense revolutionaries. So do they. After all, we identify with the poor and oppressed. So do they. How then should we react to these individuals so different from us in some ways but so alike in others? What was our judgment to be of interpreter Oanh, ambassador Minh, editor Tang, and the former schoolteacher who is North Vietnam's Prime Minister? This deeper intuitive dialogue was at work throughout our trip while at the same time, in endless conversations around a variety of tea tables, we sought to understand what it meant to speak of the "withdrawal" of American troops, the status of the N.L.F. as the "sole authentic representative" of the people of South Vietnam, and the "actual deeds" required of the United States before peace negotiations could begin.

One of the major tasks of the next generation if we are to have peace with justice, we think, will be to redefine America's interests, redefine Communism, redefine our place in the world, going beyond all conceptions inherited from the Cold War, especially beyond the concept of "the other side." We agree with North Vietnamese Prime Minister Pham Van Dong's statement to us: "The great truth of our time is that we must be brothers. The highest sentiment is fraternity. This age is the age of that sentiment." To ourselves, Pham Van Dong is not part of an "other side," but part of that great cross-section of humanity that today is emerging from misery to independence.

III

The reader will naturally wonder, How accurate was the picture of peace terms, and of Vietnamese Communism and society which we obtained? Since we both feel strongly that the United States should withdraw from Vietnam, how can we be sure that our listening and questioning was objective?

It should go without saying that as intellectuals who are not specialists in Southeast Asian affairs, as travelers for a few days in countries which were new to us and whose languages we did not know, we doubtless have made many errors of detail in our report.

What will most concern many readers, however, is not an occasional date mistaken or name misspelled, but that our

sources of information were Communist, and we had precon-
ceived feelings about the war before our journey.

In response to the understandable question as to the reliabil-
ity of our fact-finding, we should like to say that we attempted to correct for bias in ourselves and in our informants.
Each of us took full notes, and many conversations were tape-
recorded. Since we had the rare opportunity to question
North Vietnamese and National Liberation Front representatives in four Communist capitals, we attempted to check
Communist sources against each other. On return we sought to
check what we had been told against alternate sources of
information in the West: books; other travelers to both North
and South Vietnam; specialists such as Paul Mus and Jean
Lacouture; non-Communist South Vietnamese students now in
the United States.

But we also would like skeptical readers to join us in
recognizing that our Government as well as others can be
deceptive and that both sides should be heard. In *Liberation*
magazine for March, 1966, Staughton has referred to the U.S.
Government's habitual lack of veracity about Vietnam. In the
U-2 episode of 1960, in the Bay of Pigs invasion of 1961, in the
Cuba missile crisis of 1962, the American Government lied,
but its deception was temporary, episodic. What was most
dangerous was that during the missile crisis Arthur Sylvester,
then and now public relations officer for the Pentagon, said
that every government has the right to lie to preserve itself.
The fruits of Sylvesterism in Vietnam are public knowledge.
One of the reasons that during the peace offensive the other
side paid no attention to American words and watched only
American actions is that, understandably, they had lost confidence in the truth of what the American Government says.

On the whole we think the information given us was
accurate, although our hosts were superficial in describing
certain of the grimmer aspects of their revolution's history,

and guarded about aspects of their military and diplomatic situation. We were impressed that the figure for desertions from the South Vietnamese Army in 1965 presented to us in Hanoi, a statistic which the North Vietnamese would have every reason to exaggerate, quite coincided with the figure (about ten thousand a month) stated in the *New York Times* after our return. In our opinion, on matters such as these the Government of North Vietnam has at least as good a record for truth-telling as the Government of the United States.

A second, more subtle barrier to grasping the reality of this war is that Americans cut themselves off from a source of truth by deadening their emotions about it. The anthropologist Marshall Sahlins argued that Americans in Vietnam called themselves "advisers" not only because they wished to conceal United States violations of the Geneva Agreements, but also for the more intimate reason that in this way they shielded themselves from the consequences of their actions. Reflecting on conversations with American personnel in that "theater," Sahlins wrote: "To be an adviser is to be involved yet free of the place, to indulge a sense of duty yet disdain responsibility; so it becomes a prefabricated barrier erected wherever and whenever the ugliness intrudes into consciousness, a denial that one is implicated by what may be going on."[3] That state of mind is, Sahlins said, "a moral anesthetic"; we would argue further that it can interfere with finding truth. To be "detached" can mean what the word literally says, i.e., to be "out of touch." To be "objective" can mean apprehending people as if they were things. We are not prepared to agree with Presi-

[3] Marshall Sahlins, "The Destruction of Conscience in Viet Nam," *Dissent*, January–February, 1966, p. 44. For a discussion of the related myth that Diem invited us to Vietnam, see Robert Scheer, *How the United States Got Involved in Vietnam* (Santa Barbara, 1965). An American who wishes to judge his moral responsibility for what is happening in Vietnam must read Eric Norden, "American Atrocities in Vietnam," *Liberation*, February, 1966.

dent Lyndon Johnson's contention in his speech at Princeton on May 11, 1966, that the responsibility of the intellectual in confronting the question of Vietnam is to be "cool." Rather, we concur with Professor Howard Zinn's comment in the course of a defense of abolitionism that "there is no necessary connection between emotionalism and irrationality." Zinn argued that if a rational decision is a decision based on knowledge, the person who has passionately and personally involved himself in a problem may have kinds of knowledge which the detached onlooker does not.[4]

To our minds, the first-hand reporter who has feelings about what he sees (who may have taken the trouble to view at first-hand because he had feelings) can uncover truths invisible to the observer at a distance. He can help us to be objective—in the sense of seeing something in the round, from all sides, as a three-dimensional object rather than as a two-dimensional picture.

Bias takes many forms, and there is no guaranteed road to truth about the war in Vietnam. We are conscious of the ways in which some intellectuals during the nineteen-thirties sought to excuse the evil side of Soviet Communism, and we have made every effort to avoid those habits of thought. When possible, we checked the accuracy of statements made to us; in any case, those statements, from sources not often accessible to the West, are of interest in themselves. Feelings we had, but we think that those feelings helped us to be sensitive to the other side's perception of, for example, how guerrilla existence influences the building of Communism in societies like China and Vietnam.

We have tried to tell the truth without reckoning whose cause it would help or hinder.

[4] Howard Zinn, "Abolitionists, Freedom-Riders, and the Tactics of Agitation," *The Antislavery Vanguard: New Essays on the Abolitionists,* ed. Martin Duberman (Princeton, 1965), p. 428.

2

VARIETIES OF
REVOLUTIONARY EXPERIENCE I:
PRAGUE AND MOSCOW

I

We left on the evening of Sunday, December 19. A few days earlier the United States had bombed an electric power plant near Haiphong. Our trip had been scheduled for Christmas to suit Staughton's academic schedule. Now with escalation apparently imminent and talk of a Christmas truce in the air, the holiday season seemed strangely appropriate. We said in a statement released after we left the United States:

We have no assurance that we can add anything to American understanding of the other side's approach to peace. The recent bombing of Haiphong and the danger that this dreadful war may be further escalated, however, confirm us in the feeling that we should try.

As planes sped us from New York to London, London to Prague, President Johnson was initiating the peace offensive with his statement that America would knock on any door for peace, that it would not wait passively but would pursue peace relentlessly wherever the quest might lead.

It was raining in Prague when we arrived. Plowed fields came right up to the landing strips. Industrial structures, some in use and some incomplete, were in evidence as our British plane set down.

We were met by a representative of the Czech Communist Party and driven to a downtown hotel. Through the car windows appeared a city part industrialized and part medieval, with numerous ancient castles and churches dominating the skyline. A bit drab, a bit desolate, a place to work but not to live, we judged, but perhaps our judgment was influenced by the gray day or the American concepts of a city that we brought with us. In contrast to the U.S., everything seemed small: for instance, the tiny streetcars, just then experimenting with an honor system that dispensed with conductors.

Our hotel, like the city, combined the old and the new. We shared a suite whose glory was a bath with long ornate metal faucets and a tub large enough not merely for an emperor but his horse as well. The suite also had a shortwave radio and in the course of our stay we spent much time late at night listening—the programs ranged from Russian music to a B.B.C. broadcast of *The Magic Flute*—as we sought, alone and together, to cope with the anxieties of an adventure which had become real. Downstairs, the hotel lobby featured a display of the British *Worker* and its equivalents from other countries. A stroll through the streets near our hotel took us past crowded shops selling books and confections. We emerged through archways of hand-hewn stone to find, on the street corners, wooden tubs filled with live carp where homeward-bound fathers purchased their Christmas dinners.

On the first evening in Prague we were invited to a celebration of the fifth anniversary of the National Liberation Front. It was held in a symphony hall and attended by about five hundred persons, the majority Czechs although there were a few Vietnamese and Africans. The program began with two short addresses, one by the vice-chairman of the Czech National Assembly, the other by Professor Nguyen Van Hieu, the Prague representative of the N.L.F. The Czech official reiterated his country's support for the N.L.F., and Professor Hieu declared his movement's determination to continue, adding an announcement of a Christmas cease-fire. Several hours of entertainment followed including chamber music of both countries, its formal delicacy a peculiarly moving way of expressing solidarity, and relaxed folk dancing and singing. The program was partly dedicated to the Czech hero Fŭcik, a poet, nationalist, and Communist, who was imprisoned and finally killed by the Nazis. (In an attempt to break his will and make him talk, the Nazis drove him around Prague, showed him the city streets where citizens conducted business-as-usual, and asked, "Where are the people demonstrating for Fŭcik?")

Both of us were deeply affected by the evening. It had not occurred to us that revolution would celebrate itself in this way. The Communist reputation is for tedious oratory and wooden pronouncement of greetings, but the reality was that of dance. In contrast, cultural support for the American effort in South Vietnam is on a show-business basis, although American entertainers with serious artistic purposes increasingly are supporting the anti-war movement. The real parallels with the celebration in Prague, we think, are the refusal of Robert Lowell and Arthur Miller to take part in cultural events sponsored by the Johnson Administration; the "read-in" movement which began at Carnegie Hall in New York on February 20; and Joan Baez leading "We Shall Overcome" as thousands marched from the Washington Monument to the Capitol, at the first mass protest in America against the war.

II

The next morning, December 21, we had a hurriedly arranged meeting with the N.L.F. delegation in its offices. The suite was not as grand as an embassy but was something more than an organizational headquarters. As Czech and Vietnamese hostesses brought in food and drink, and people moved up and down the corridor on business, we spent perhaps an hour closeted with Professor Hieu. During the interview, we had our first taste of the sweet red and dry white liqueurs the Vietnamese always offered us, and the lengthy but seriously intended toasts that began, punctuated, and ended every meeting.

Hieu's dress was Western, his manner relaxed and suave. At first glance there was little to suggest his reputation among Western scholars as the most powerful and most rigidly Leftist of the Front's personnel outside Vietnam. The pamphlet *Personalities of the South Vietnam National Liberation Front*, issued by the N.L.F. Commission for Foreign Relations, stated that Hieu is a member of the N.L.F. Central Committee, Secretary-General of the South Vietnam Peace Committee, and head of the permanent mission of the N.L.F. to Czechoslovakia and East Germany. He was born in South Vietnam in 1922, studied in Saigon and Hanoi. He wrote anti-colonial material under the pseudonym Khai Minh. In 1958 he left Saigon to go to the liberated areas. He has led N.L.F. delegations to foreign countries "on numerous occasions."[1]

[1] Bernard Fall called Hieu an "erstwhile secretary general" who now serves the N.L.F. as "roving ambassador"; his replacement as secretary-

Acknowledging the introductions, Hieu stressed that he was impressed with our coming and with the peace movement among the American people. Immediately, he gave us more details on the cease-fire. He said the U.S. called it a "proposal" but in fact it was a routine and unilateral Front practice on both Christmas and Tet, the Buddhist Lunar New Year. Vietnamese who live in the Saigon-controlled areas are permitted to visit relatives in liberated areas provided they do not carry weapons or "spy apparatus." U.S. prisoners, he added, are "moved" by the fact that the N.L.F. has Christmas celebrations for them.

He questioned us about the U.S. peace movement, and we three took turns giving our impressions of it. During our description of the November 27 March on Washington, we mentioned the speech by the president of the Students for a Democratic Society, Carl Oglesby, and Hieu said one of his few English words: "SDS, SDS."

Arrangements for our travel beyond Prague were made

---

general by Huynh Tan Phat "was said to have been a concession to the more moderate elements of the Front." (Bernard Fall, "Viet-Cong—The Unseen Enemy in Viet-Nam," *The Viet-Nam Reader*, ed. Marcus G. Raskin and Bernard B. Fall [New York, 1965], p. 259).

Malcolm Browne wrote: "Western intelligence specialists speculate that the greatest power in the Viet Cong politburo belongs to its secretary general, a former mathematics teacher named Nguyen Van Hieu. Hieu is certainly the best-known Viet Cong leader outside South Viet Nam. Besides his politburo duties, he is a kind of shadow foreign minister and ambassador without portfolio for the Front, lecturing and attending ceremonies in Indonesia, Czechoslovakia, East Germany, the Soviet Union, China and other communist or nonaligned countries. He seems to get in and out of South Viet Nam without difficulty." (Malcolm Browne, *The New Face of War* [Indianapolis and New York, 1965], p. 241).

In June, 1966, Staughton was told by an associate of Professor Hieu's that the latter had given up his post and returned to Vietnam. In September, 1966, when Charles De Gaulle visited Cambodia, Hieu was there as the N.L.F. representative.

through North Vietnamese Ambassador Phan Van Su. This man works in a real embassy with several rooms on two floors and a large staff. In a spacious sunlit parlor, under a painting of Ho Chi Minh, we exchanged greetings. This interview was difficult because it had to be translated from Vietnamese or English through Czech.

The ambassador was an older man than Professor Hieu, thin, with a lined face, and quite dignified. He and his interpreter said that they both were from South Vietnam and had not seen or heard from their families since 1954. "We do not know if they are alive or dead. That is why normalization of mail service between North and South, which to you may seem a small thing, is not small to us."

The evening of December 21 we attended a reception which had been prepared by the Vietnamese students in Prague. Perhaps two hundred people were there, including Czechs and Africans. It was strange, watching the well-dressed men and women standing in line at the coat-check counter or chatting around the buffet, to think: This is the enemy. We moved awkwardly through the crowded room, now and then nodding and smiling to the D.R.V. ambassador or Professor Hieu, and finally sat down at one of the small tables near the wall. Then the N.L.F. interpreter whom we had met that morning appeared. He joined us at our table, seemingly out of courtesy, but as we talked, it became the first substantial conversation we had had with a Vietnamese.

The interpreter was young, slight, and intelligent. He made it clear that the other side's negotiating positions had been officially set forth in the Four Points of D.R.V. Prime Minister Pham Van Dong's speech of April 8, 1965, and the Five Points declared by the N.L.F. in March. His informal summary of the other side's position was: respect the Geneva Agreements, stop the aggressive war, pull out U.S. troops, dismantle U.S. bases, and stop bombing the North; respect Vietnamese national rights, accept the principle that the internal affairs of the South Vietnamese should be settled by them alone; the N.L.F. is the sole genuine representative of South Vietnam and should have a decisive voice in any settlement there.

We raised the question of how a new government in South Vietnam might be created, since the issue is not covered by the Geneva Agreements. He emphasized that there were "many ways and means" through negotiation among various South Vietnamese groups. But, he said, there would have to be common ground among these groups, namely common opposition to U.S. aggression. Even officers of the puppet Government and Army could participate, he said, provided they renounce their past. If the N.L.F. plans to create a government with groups not in the N.L.F. at present, he asked, how could it now lay out a concrete plan?

He stressed that the N.L.F. view of the South Vietnamese government of the future is a concession: Geneva called for reunification by 1956, whereas the N.L.F. today envisions a neutralist, coalition government in South Vietnam for an indefinite period before reunification of North and South. "Why should we not make concessions, many people ask us, just so to spare the blood of our people. But my leaders would not spare any means that really leads to our goals." On the issue of an election in the South, the interpreter said: "Not fixed yet. This should be decided through common efforts. Maybe Secretary [of State Dean] Rusk worries too much about our people. I believe that in the bottom of his heart Secretary Rusk believes the N.L.F. will keep its words. So far we have."

He displayed a remarkable ability to view from different

political angles, to understand the colonizer as well as the anti-colonials. "Speaking as a Vietnamese, I would say: even if the sky falls after American withdrawal, even so, that would be only a question for Vietnamese. But putting myself in the place of an American peace worker, realities in South Vietnam show that the bloodshed and disorder have been caused by the U.S. intervention. If people have been arrested, killed, and tortured, it is by America or by its puppets. A lot about this has even been said in the U.S. press itself."

The interpreter concluded: "Many of our participants were not Communists at first. Still the President of the N.L.F. is a non-Party intellectual. But the harsher the repression, the more they became Communists. You Americans are making Communists."

III

Wednesday, December 22, our last morning in Prague, we drove out to Lidice, the little village of one thousand inhabitants which was wiped out in 1942 by the Nazis in retaliation for the assassination of Protector Reinhard Heydrich. It had been a center of militant strikes by the coal miners and was representative of the strong national tradition in the villages. It was here, perhaps more than at Guernica, that the modern terror began. Simply to teach a lesson to all nationalist Czechs, the Nazis burned down all the houses, stores, churches, and other buildings. They shot all the men whom they found, waited for the others to come up from the mines, then shot them too. The women were sent to Ravensbrueck, the children to "reeducation camps." The Nazis attempted altogether to liquidate the village—to prove that history can be changed by force, that existence can become nothingness. When the world heard of the incident, there was extensive mourning. In the United States as in other countries, many expressed their sadness with concrete gestures. Following the Allied victory in the war, international brigades of students came and rebuilt the destroyed town. The women of Lidice who survived were liberated from the concentration camps, and some of the children came home. A search began for every remaining relic of the village. Charred pieces of a church door, bone fragments, identification cards of the miners were found. A museum was erected to house these relics, and the women included in it the remains of their Ravensbrueck uniforms, the official Nazi documents ordering the execution of the villagers, and gifts received from well-wishers everywhere. Beyond the museum was erected a beautiful arch with the single word "peace" suspended in its dome. Nearby is a rose garden, built with stones from all over the world, particularly from countries which lost whole cities in the war. It might have been the cemetery of an era, for etched in stone were the words: Lidice, Coventry, Hiroshima, Nagasaki.

Tom wrote later: "I couldn't help thinking that the women who guided us through the museum—it was closed but they opened it for us, and showed movies of the destruction and rebuilding of the village—were survivors of Ravensbrueck. They were strong in their movements, aged in appearance, courteous to us, but withdrawn. I wanted badly to take one by the arm and ask if we could talk about all she remembers; but it was just impossible to summon the nerve, or crush the feeling that it would have been inhumanly awkward to open the subject. I clamped down the desire to say to one of them: Perhaps my experience is simply too small to embrace what has happened here, but you must know that many others in my country have not learned very much in twenty-five years since we wept over Lidice. Even now we three must go to another small country where villages are being burned to teach people a 'lesson.' You must know that. How can you bear it and live here? I could not; it is too much."[2]

IV

Conversations during our last few hours in Prague brought us face-to-face with the great debate in world Communism about coexistence between capitalism and socialism. It would be the main theme of our shorter stay in Moscow, too.

The West is well aware that this debate concerns domestic as well as foreign policy in the Communist societies. Indeed, the premise of the strategy of containment-and-détente, developed by George F. Kennan, W. W. Rostow, the late President John F. Kennedy, and their co-thinkers, is that as Communist societies industrialize their foreign policies will become more peaceable. When living standards rise, they theorize, the apocalyptic vision of worldwide revolution pales and Communists turn bourgeois. Thus in the Far East, by this formula, Chinese Communism is now young and aggressive; all revolutions in the area can be assumed to be Peking-inspired, and must be militantly combated; but later, when Mao Tse-tung and his generation are dead and China is affluent, peace may be possible.

[2] While we were in Hanoi, the 173rd Airborne Brigade carried out the following operation near the Cambodia border:
"Armed HU-1B helicopters poured 3,000 rockets into villages that used to harbor the Vietcong. They burned to the ground every hut they could find. Sampans were sunk and bullock carts were smashed. . . . Some 700 civilians—women, children, and old men—were removed from the area to resettlement camps. . . . Every cooking utensil was smashed, every banana tree severed, every mattress slashed." (Associated Press dispatch from Saigon, January 6, 1966, quoted by *National Guardian,* January 22, 1966).

It was a fascinating introduction to the controversy which rages between North Vietnam's two great allies to hear the views of a Czech student and a Czech professor on bourgeoisification, democratization, sophistication, pacification, corruption, the definition of the subject depending on one's point of view.

After returning from Lidice, Tom talked for over an hour with our Czech interpreter. Thirty-one, educated in Moscow, he works now in the foreign embassy. Interested in U.S. student movements, he expressed his confusion about the existence of anti-Communism within the peace movement. He had no sense of the differences between student and traditional peace groups on this issue.

He also discussed at length the present ferment in the Czech universities, reporting that there is considerable reaction against official orthodoxy. Professors are caught between the regime, which counts on them for dissemination of doctrine, and the students, who are questioning established theory and policy. Asked what policies simply cannot be challenged safely, he mentioned in particular coexistence. No one can directly challenge this thesis, he said, though some intellectuals deal with the problem by accepting the coexistence framework and then giving support to particular aspects of Chinese policy.

What concerned him most, perhaps, was a prevailing discrimination against students because of what he called the "workers' mystique." Until the nineteen-fifties, he said, students were considered "immature parasites." Even today, students who graduate from college are paid less than "simple workers." Status within the Government and Party is distributed on the same basis. He said the policy is causing "extreme reaction" among the young people, but that probably a new balance of priorities can be worked out within the present system.

Western in appearance and dress, he obviously wanted some of the rewards associated with professional status. But to classify him as bourgeois would be too simple. After all, what he was demanding has a basis in reality: technically trained students are people with certain skills. They are not by nature inferior to workers and peasants. This young man spent time in factories with working people in accordance with the Government's program, and came away with a mixed picture of workers that he could not square with Party doctrine. "Some are lazy," he said. His resentment is great; the phrases "rigid" and "old" cropped up continually in his references to the Party and Government.

We lunched and spent part of the afternoon with a Czech professor who edits a journal on international politics. A man perhaps in his mid-fifties, urbane, silver haired, he relaxed at a well-furnished hotel in an affluent city as he pondered the basis for unity in the world Communist movement. What can "solidarity" mean, we wondered, among Communists so far apart as the Czechs and Vietnamese? By what means does this professor, living comfortably in a stable society, identify his vital needs with those of the liberation forces in South Vietnam?

As the conversation unfolded, it became clear that the professor was one who accepted the general approach of his Party and the Soviets on questions of policy, although occasionally taking a controversial stand on specific issues. For example, he had written an article disagreeing with the postwar Soviet policy of taking resources from Russia's neighbor, East Germany, on the pretense of strengthening the Soviet role as leader of the international revolution. The professor thought the Soviet motive was national interest, and said so in criticism. But he remained sympathetic to the "Western" bloc in the Communist world.

Staughton asked the professor whether or not coexistence

requires the American protest movement to cooperate with so-called "rational elements" of the U.S. Establishment in order to foster good relations with the Soviet Union at the expense of trying to change the U.S. by supporting more radical groups both within the country and around the world. The professor answered: "The principle of supporting liberation movements does not mean that any movement, any time, in any region ought to be supported. I would try to give priority to whatever gets the best effect from the historically longer viewpoint. We can imagine in particular cases, direct support to a movement might be detrimental to the working class, for instance, in places where the movement starts in conditions that are so unfavorable that the action is bound to provoke countermeasures which are fundamentally damaging. I am against any action that has so little chance that it might create its opposite as a result. This becomes more the case as progressive movements grow and their responsibilities grow."

We asked if this did not often mean refusing support to movements that might be successful: for example, did not Soviet underestimation of the possibility of revolution in Cuba and China amount to quite serious error? He admitted these were both "mistakes due to applying the Marxian analysis to situations where we have a limited experience," but he said the Chinese are worse at prediction and narrower in experience than "we" are. A "margin for error" needs to be built into Marxism to allow for difficulties. These difficulties, he enumerated, include, first, the mistakes made in the effort to build a new society with the inherited relationships among people from the old order; second, mistakes due to people being people, a "mess" caused by power-seekers; and third, mistakes caused by the hostile situation: by enemies who "also decide for you what is possible."

He returned to the problem of judging ripe conditions for revolution. "Lenin and Trotsky always thought that Russia was on the outskirts of the center of revolution, Europe. Nevertheless a revolution was made in Russia, and it was twenty-five years before the revolution took the direction Lenin wanted. So, not only was Lenin unsure if Russia was the center, but also he avoided becoming impatient and depressed. Today the U.S. is the center of imperialism, but under what conditions can it be attacked? Lenin's theory was that the system could be attacked at its weak links, switching from his conception of revolution in the strong point or heart of the system. Can you have a go at the center, or must you go step by step?"

Perhaps, we speculated, the Czechs "made" their revolution too easily for them to understand the Vietnamese who were making theirs virtually without support from the Great Powers of the Communist world. Thus possibly stability seemed a more natural value to the professor while struggle would seem more natural to the Chinese and Vietnamese.

It was difficult to judge with so little time, but our guess would be that the professor and the Vietnamese can be allies. Like the younger man who had gone with us to Lidice, the professor expressed disgust about imperial wars in small countries, and for him to abandon the Vietnamese would mean very nearly abandoning Marxism. But if there is solidarity, it will be among people who greatly differ as well. Not simply are there East-West, white-colored differences but also differences at every cultural and educational level. In the streets of Prague, many of the young people dress and wear their hair in unmistakable Beatle fashion; in Hanoi the only "youth rebellion" that we found centered around new forms of verse. In Prague full houses watch *After the Fall*, Arthur Miller's play, which records the decline of Utopian faith into corruption; in Hanoi full houses applaud the story of Nguyen Van Troi, the young man who was executed for attempting to kill Defense Secretary Robert S. McNamara.

V

This contrast between Western or stable Communism, and Eastern or struggling Communism, presented itself much more sharply in Moscow. We arrived at the great international airport there late on the evening of Wednesday, December 22, and we left only twenty-four hours later for Peking. Into the intervening time we packed successive interviews with the North Vietnamese ambassador, the permanent representative of the National Liberation Front, and the members of the Soviet Peace Committee. Particularly striking was our Moscow interview with the Front.

Dang Quang Minh was the second major N.L.F. leader whom we met on the journey. He is a member of the Front Central Committee and head of its permanent mission to the U.S.S.R. Minh was born in 1909, Hieu, the Front representative whom we met in Prague, in 1922. Both are former teachers, but Minh seems to have suffered far more directly than Hieu in the Resistance. Minh has been a revolutionist since 1927, was first imprisoned by the French in 1930, then arrested again in 1940 and not released until the 1945 revolution from his cell in the "most terrible prison," Poulo Condor. From 1954 to 1960 he worked in the South Vietnamese peace movement, then went to the liberated areas and became a member of the N.L.F. Central Committee at its Second Congress.

Minh's style of discourse was arresting: a soft tone, some-times nearly inaudible, precision with ideas, great care in covering every significant point, deep patience coupled with a low-keyed intensity about making us understand. He spoke ideologically, rather than adopting the stance of an experi-enced diplomat, and we were aware that the wisdom of forty years was being sifted in our presence.

The only time we saw D.R.V. and N.L.F. personnel overlap occurred during this interview. Shortly after our conversation began—it was clear that the translations were difficult—the better interpreter from the D.R.V. embassy arrived to trans-late for us. He, like the N.L.F. interpreter in Prague, was a young, bespectacled, intellectual-appearing man.

Greeting us, Minh said: "We consider South Vietnam to be in the front line and the American people to be in the rear of one struggle. The American people are inside the enemy's ranks."

He proceeded to speak of "the maneuvers of the U.S. Government in South Vietnam, and the objectives of our struggle—how to defeat the U.S."

"The strategy of the U.S. is to occupy South Vietnam and turn it into a new kind of colony. The struggle is, according to the N.L.F., not to let the U.S. turn South Vietnam into its military base, its new kind of colony.

"The demand is the withdrawal of all U.S. troops, the destruction of all U.S. military bases in South Vietnam so as to win our national independence. We must have real national independence, real peace in South Vietnam. We will carry out a policy of neutrality and afterward realize national reunifica-tion. If the U.S. still is occupying South Vietnam, we have not yet gained freedom, sovereignty, democracy, and cannot seek reunification.

"The South Vietnamese people could not agree if there is any base or unit of the U.S., no matter how small it may be. If a small base, it is temporary, to prepare a new attack.

"Our fundamental problem is how to prevent a U.S. occupation.

"If now the U.S. Government has to withdraw, but leaves a part of its troops there, what would be the aim? It means they have not given up their scheme to occupy South Vietnam. Because if the U.S. could occupy South Vietnam, then the South Vietnamese people would have to undergo still greater sufferings than they have since 1956. North Vietnam would be directly threatened by this, too; the danger of an expanded war would increase if the U.S. could occupy South Vietnam. Also if the U.S. could occupy, then the peace of the world would be threatened."

We asked about America's saving face. "When the U.S. aggressors started this aggression, they unmasked themselves, they lost their face. It is not up to South Vietnam to save their face. They should cease aggression, then their face will be saved.

"Those who defend the heroic U.S. traditions of Lincoln and Washington, these are not the aggressors.

"The question in South Vietnam is that the U.S. must withdraw. They have to withdraw from other parts of the world too. The experiment of so-called special war is being defeated in South Vietnam. The U.S. imperialists want to carry out an experiment to launch a counteroffensive against national independence in the world. Their withdrawal would mean a big defeat for the imperialists and a big victory for the people of the world. This is a life-and-death question for imperialists.

"If now the South Vietnamese people are in the twentieth

year of struggle, and are enjoying wide support, if we let the U.S. stay, it would not open up any prospects for people in the world struggling for their independence.

"But this is the era of collapsing colonial systems and the era of a series of victories for national liberation movements. The struggle of the South Vietnamese people will lead to the collapse of the colonial system in that part of the world.

"In other words, the revolutionary forces are the strongest and the U.S. is in a stalemated situation. We are sure we will win the war, but we limit our victory to chasing the aggressors out of South Vietnam.

"The U.S. still hopes to stay in South Vietnam. They must become hopeless. The U.S. sees the failure of special war and escalation, but they are still not yet hopeless because they have not realized the force of a people's war. They are still hoping to improvise a victory by expanding the war.

"They are boasting about the U.S. willingness to carry out negotiations, with the aim of putting pressure on South Vietnam to negotiate under conditions which compel the South Vietnamese people to surrender. We think the people of the world do not agree that the South Vietnamese should lay down their arms and surrender.

"Generally, we have put forward our aims lower than the possibilities. This [concession] is to some extent a face-saving device for the U.S.

"Concretely the people are stronger than in 1954 at Dienbienphu. Not only because of our own forces, but because of the support of the people in the world. We may say that in 1954 the support of the world was not so strong as today. We may say that the coordinated struggle of the French with our people then is not as strong as the coordinated struggle of Americans with our people today. We say this because we have to consider the difficulties and advantages of France then and the U.S. today. Although the French movement was very strong, it was not as wide and embracing of as many strata as in the U.S. movement today. The workers' movement was strong, but other strata were not as strong in France. But the U.S. people are fighting under harder conditions than the French. From the point of view of forms of struggle, those in America are rich and varied. Every form, from the simplest such as burning draft cards, up to the act of burning oneself. On the other side, never before among the ruling circles has there been so much contradiction. In the history of the U.S. there has never been a government so opposed by the people and isolated as the Johnson Government. Many people are not supporting our struggle but they are against the Johnson policy. Internationally, Johnson only gets the direct support of fourteen countries. France, for example, is ready to make use of a U.S. defeat; and although the United Kingdom is supporting the U.S., it has not contributed very effectively. A worldwide front is now shaping.

"Our demands are lower than those put forward in 1954. For instance, the Geneva Agreements didn't put forward a political program for South Vietnam. Now the N.L.F. puts forward a program of neutrality. Also the Geneva Conference defined ways of reunification, but the N.L.F. has not put forward forms of national reunification. We say let it be decided by the two zones. Also the Geneva Conference did not provide for a coalition government in the South, but the N.L.F. has. The N.L.F. program is very rational. We could never give up these aims because they are lower than 1954. We will win victories by very rational ways, and we are certain that people will agree with us. But the American imperialists are still not going to give up. That is why the South Vietnamese people have no other way than arms.

"The South Vietnamese people cherish peace more than any people in the world. As you know, for twenty-five years the South Vietnamese people have been living in war.

"But when we are fighting we continue to build our country. Free zones now are four-fifths of the territory. War cannot prevent people in the free zones from building a new life. Agricultural production, education, and cultural affairs are proceeding very well. We are reeducating collaborators to come back to the people. One example of our work you could not imagine. In the past five years, we helped fourteen minorities who had no script; now they do. Life in the liberated zones is higher than during the Resistance against the French. If now the war would be banished, we could concentrate on building a new life for all. Who doesn't want this?

"Another way to win the war is through long-term resistance. The U.S. still is not hopeless. In this we can both fight and build up. The more we fight the stronger we become, the weaker become the Americans.

"Monopolists don't mind sending planes. But they mind their sons going to this war. They could never send enough to reoccupy the liberated zones. From the technical point of view, we compel hand-to-hand fighting. They are not used to it. We could wipe out whole battalions with insignificant casualties. U.S. modern weapons cannot be used. On the contrary, when we capture their weapons, they can be fully used. There are limits on the U.S. because the war is in a colonial agricultural country.

"The U.S. can withdraw or drag on losing. In our own opinion they have no possibility of gaining the upper hand to negotiate. The day will come when they must withdraw.

"We cannot talk with you about concrete conditions because the day has not come. Before discussion of concrete conditions we must make the U.S. hopeless and agree to withdraw. It is not yet realistic to discuss concrete conditions. You may say they would divert our struggle.

"On coalition government afterward, we cannot talk about coalition concretely. But in general, it should embrace representatives of all patriotic mass organizations and individuals who are opposing the aggressive war. It does not mean the government would not embrace former collaborators. We have examples.

"It is not yet realistic to discuss the steps toward forming a new government. After forming a coalition government, the social and economic program is for the future; but during the past few years the N.L.F. has had a program: our agrarian reform has given two million hectares of land to individual peasants. There has been increasing agricultural production. We are building, in spite of devastation, and we are flourishing.

"The people of the U.S. are victims of this war also."

As we rose to leave, this quiet man clasped our hands long and hard.

3

VARIETIES OF
REVOLUTIONARY EXPERIENCE II:
PEKING

I

We landed in Peking early in the afternoon of December 24. The sense of a different world was immediate. It was cold and clear, something like the weather back in New Haven and Newark, but there the similarity ceased. We could feel that the West was behind us, and here we were pulled toward a variety of new faces, sounds, motions. The Communist "Internationale" boomed with conviction from outdoor loudspeakers at the large modern airport. A delegation of Vietnamese met us, and we were driven the several miles to the city, past bicyclists, donkey carts, buses, and groups of workers in the expansive fields by the roadside.

At our hotel we learned that no plane would travel to Hanoi until Monday, December 27. Even then, since the Hanoi airport is not large enough for jets and the bi-weekly plane from Peking has only twenty-four seats, it was uncertain if there would be room for us. We spent Christmas in our cottagelike quarters in the heart of municipal Peking.

Several times we journeyed out into the streets. Sometimes we walked alone, sometimes as a group, and less frequently with guides through this strange new world. When Tom went out in the evening, he took with him a note from the hotel manager, in Chinese, explaining who he was and where he should be returned if lost. The note was never needed.

The streets of Peking are clean, and piles of coal are left for the residents to heat their small houses. For the most part these dwellings are of clay or stone, with a few rooms, one-story high, connected around little courtyards. Markets and shops are scattered here and there, as are schools, small factories, squares, and official buildings.

People on foot or bicycle seem to move endlessly down these streets, and in the many hours we walked among them we never saw an accident or incident. It is too simple to say, as many do, that Peking is a city of conformity. True, most people wear the convenient and inexpensive blue quilted suit, although other colors appear as well. True again, the sheer number of people in the streets suggests a mass society. But there are so many varieties: the high-cheeked Mongolian sitting cross-legged atop his cartload of cabbages; the round-faced unarmed police girl directing traffic; the soldier in his olive uniform with red star, scanning the newspaper on the wall; the teen-agers playing basketball in the courtyard of their school as we stroll down a nearby alley. Everywhere is the pulse of purposeful activity. Walking before breakfast one day, we passed a group of women energetically singing before starting the day's work. Later, in Wuhan, our airport bus passed at six in the morning group after group of young soldiers jogging along the roadside to keep fit.

Despite our color, never did we encounter visible hostility as we walked, night and day, through Peking. In one store where Tom struggled to explain that he wanted a sweater, the saleswoman sent him down the street to a bank to exchange currency. At the bank when Tom finished the transaction he tried, despite embarrassment, to say he was an American in order to discover the response. The girl behind the counter smiled and said, calmly and clearly: "Yes, we distinguish between the aggressive policy and the American people."

The new Peking is stunning. We rode down the widest boulevard we had ever seen, past old colonial buildings converted into embassies or new state offices. We stopped to watch ice-skating on the pond at the university, whose campus rivals any in America for physical charm. Construction was universal: public housing, roads, canals. We walked awed across Tien An Men Square, "Gate of Heavenly Peace," where the towering museum and public buildings overlook grounds where thousands upon thousands can gather for rallies.

The first person who met us was twenty-six-year-old Phan Doan Nam from the North Vietnamese embassy, who handled the details of our stay. Fluent in English after four years of study at Moscow University, he now rarely returns to Vietnam. Like the others we met, he welcomed us with thanks for the "strong movement" in the United States, and we felt obliged to explain its modest size. Nam, we learned, has a cynical sense of humor akin to that of civil rights activists. "There are not many Americans in the Northern part of our country," he said, "but there are many visiting the South." He added: "We have to watch that they do not attack us while we are observing their Christmas holiday." He clearly took a militant line toward the war. The French, he thought, "did nothing" about peace until beaten at Dienbienphu, and Hanoi now should show no sign of interest in peace until the American will is broken. He joked about the American charge of

North Vietnamese "infiltration," calling it a refusal to admit "there is a mass uprising in the South." When the war ends, Premier Nguyen Cao Ky and the others would escape the country rather than become part of the solution: "It is not for us to give them the opportunity, but they will flee." He viewed the National Liberation Front as a broad coalition, but stressed the need for its base among the peasants and workers. "Some used to believe that North Vietnamese Communism makes everything common, but experience is showing them differently. Our line is independent. It is based on the reality of Vietnam. Only the Vietnamese know what must be done in Vietnam. So, too, China acts in accord with her own situation."

II

Herbert had been welcome in Prague and Moscow because of the American Communist Party's support for the Soviet Union in its dispute with Peking. We presumed, however, that Peking knew Herbert's identification with the Soviet stand, and we feared the Chinese might view our trip with suspicion. This expectation appeared confirmed when no Chinese met us at the airport. However, our Vietnamese hosts called the Chinese Peace Committee after delivering us to the Peace Hotel, and soon there appeared for what would prove to be the longest and most frank talks of our journey, our interpreters and guides, Tang Ming-chao and Gao Hsien.

They put us at ease rapidly by expressing their pleasure at the opportunity to "discuss our views" and by inviting us to dinner that evening. We noticed that in the initial discussion Tang Ming-chao repeatedly emphasized his country's flexibility and experimentalism, as if anticipating that we would have an image of Chinese dogmatism.

Tang, the senior member of the team, did most of the talking, in an animated and fluent English which he had developed in the thirties as a graduate student at the University of California. Tang said of Vietnam: "Most don't realize that many Vietnamese took part in the Chinese Revolution. I was in North Vietnam last November and my interpreter there had fought in the Chinese Army." In one of his many knowledgeable comments about the U.S., he asked Herbert to give greetings to his daughter, Bettina, now an avowed Communist student leader at Berkeley. In addition to the Berkeley experience, Tang could list several years' residence in the Greenwich Village district of Manhattan as part of his background. In every way his manners were those of a cosmopolitan, able to move gracefully in any society of the world. Currently he serves as a secretary of the Chinese Peace Committee and an editor of the Western-oriented magazine *China Reconstructs*. We were not the first Americans he had hosted; Tang was among the Chinese who met Edgar Snow when he came to collect material for his book, *The Other Side of the River*. He also was an early member of the Chinese Revolution, first taking part in protests in the nineteen-twenties.

Gao Hsien, a younger man perhaps in his thirties, was pleasant and, though lacking Tang's experience, had learned about the United States in considerable detail. He surprised Tom while we strolled through the Chinese Revolutionary Museum by asking if the anti-war activities of Students for a Democratic Society were harming its community organizing projects. As we were to feel over and over throughout the trip, we three Americans were woefully new and awkward before these faraway people who know so much about our country.

That first evening we went with Tang and Gao to dinner. They called for us in a black Chinese limousine, one of the few cars which we saw, as automobiles are available only for "official purposes." We drove in the dusk across Peking, moving slowly and honking constantly in the midst of crowds of people on foot or bicycle going home. Finally, we arrived at the restaurant, a one-story maze of rooms and patios. As in the other Chinese restaurants we visited, we were escorted to a separate room where we could talk easily while eating; but, we were told, the restaurants are open to all, food is the same for everyone, and prices are low.

At the beginning of our conversations, which would continue for several hours and be resumed on our return from Hanoi, Tang stressed his deep interest in Chinese domestic problems, particularly that of educating the younger generation to maintain the traditional line of Chinese revolutionary policies. Only after leaving China did it become apparent to us that these discussions were preoccupying the Chinese leadership as a whole. Our dialogue was prelude to the great controversies which China would air publicly a few months later. Official Chinese organs now polemicize against "bourgeois" or "revisionist" thinking among certain intellectuals, journalists, and professionals within the country. These "revisionists," whose political base was in the Peking municipal government and the university, officials charged, favor slower collectivization with greater private landholding, economic cooperation with the Soviet Union and the West, and peaceful evolution in foreign policy.

As we would learn, the relation between the Chinese younger generation and the Vietnam war is a close one, for Vietnam represents the nearby "school" from which young Chinese are developing their attitudes toward the United States. "Our generation went through a Revolution; but the younger generation, what does it know?" Tang asked. China has been free of struggle on its own territory for more than eighteen years, and the new generation sees, not Japanese occupation forces, but new schools, factories, and housing developments that promise an easier and richer future than earlier generations have known. Everywhere in Peking the old society is being replaced by the new. Alongside the prevalent small dwellings four- and five-story "projects" similar to those in the United States are being built. (We were told the architects are furiously debating the relative merits of the efficiency of large projects against the more humane values embodied in smaller-scale units.) The point is that progress is everywhere. Millions of Chinese are involved in its creation. In Peking we saw thousands of people digging a canal while music blared from outdoor loudspeakers; in Wuhan, an industrial city in central China, we crossed over the Yangtze River on a great bridge that was constructed in two years; the smaller factories carry on them a painted red star, as if to say: this may seem small at present, but at least it is ours and is growing daily. This is the reality which young people know, and it made Tang wonder about the future.

"We could become capitalist," he said, shaking his head. "We could go the way of Yugoslavia and the Soviet Union," where, he argued, individual incentives of a "bourgeois" variety have been built into the political economy.

"Take India, for example, where people starve in the streets. A little girl here looks at a picture of starving Indian people and asks, 'Why don't they go to the dining hall?' The little girl does not understand why there is no dining hall. She has no experience with class struggle."

He predicted the fearful course a rising generation could take. "The children of the people who are in office now, the intellectuals, Party people, engineers, and so forth, these children are born with a silver spoon in the mouth. They are the first generation to be literate. Since they are from a semi-bourgeois group they do better in school than children of workers and peasants. If you are mechanical about the educational system, these kids will pass on until they are sitting on top of the mass of people. Then they begin to invent concepts such as 'natural rights' or 'special privileges' to suit themselves. They begin to want peace, not to want revolutionary struggles in other countries."

To combat the problem of such a privileged class, the Chinese are introducing new systems of education and labor in which workers and peasants attend school part-time, and professional or "bourgeois" people spend part of their careers performing manual labor, or working among the people in factories of the countryside. Tang's wife, he said, was completing six months of work in a Chinese village, and his two daughters were engaged in part-time factory work as they attended school.

We remembered the long discussion in Prague with the young Czech interpreter who so frankly complained of the straitjacket system imposed in the forties and fifties, the system which insisted that manual labor be performed by students, that workers' wage scales be higher than the starting pay for young professionals, that all the country should honor the proletarian mystique and disdain the bourgeois. The result, reported our Czech friend, was resentment, bordering on revolt, against Party and state among the newer generation desiring the mobility and status of the Western middle classes.

We asked Tang if this could happen in China, either because of the temptations of affluence, or through a typical conflict of generations? Is it possible, we questioned, to impose a style and system of values on a whole people without incurring rebellions among very creative elements? Would the Chinese leadership take the risk of giving the younger generation a choice of futures?

His answer was so abrupt as to indicate misunderstanding, or to suggest a desire not to speculate on the possibility of such changes. "These young people shouldn't become a group unto themselves," he said, "but instead must become part of the people."

Asked for concrete examples, he listed a wide variety of opportunities for privileges open to Chinese officials. "A commune director: unless you are politically good, there are many opportunities to be corrupt. You might promote inequality, assigning good jobs to people you like, bad jobs to people you don't. Distribution can be rigged too. You can bribe local judges, police, Party secretaries, even form a black market. Under socialism where you can't manipulate stocks, still the managers can control the factories despite the existence of supervisory bodies. Lenin pointed out the spontaneous development of capitalism within socialist societies: there is corruption of all forms, and once a man has tasted it without being caught, he becomes much bolder."

Only a "socialist education campaign" can be effective in preventing these corrupt growths, Tang insisted. "We cannot rely on the courts or police, but only on the people, to catch the dirt and clean it up. The people must be educated to socialism. There can be no special privileges: ordinary school, ordinary clothing, equal transportation. Everyone must work: my daughter works two weeks of every three months in a factory; my eleven-year-old just finished two weeks of working in a shop. They identify with workers. At vacation time they go out in the countryside to the farms."

Corruption and unsettled grievances cannot be discovered by managers or others outside the work force, he went on. "If you call a meeting and ask the men what their grievances are, they won't tell you. But if you work with them on a machine, they will tell you much. My wife has been in a province for six months; she has mobilized the people, she has exposed the contradiction of favoritism among people there."

As to the use of punishment to correct practices, Tang voiced an understanding of its shortcomings. "When we criticize, we criticize severely; but in dealing with problems, we must be mild. When a person is mistaken, it usually is what we call an honest mistake that anyone can make. Less than one percent of the people are really bad, and those we remove from their jobs. But even if fired, they still receive pay. That is the worst that can happen here."[1]

He acknowledged the use of limited material incentives in the economy—"More skillful people get an improvement in salary"—but called the process a modest and slow one, with most accumulated funds going into new investment. The wage system has not changed drastically since the days of the Revolution when everyone received the same pay. "In peacetime we ask, what should we do? We sent some people to the Soviet Union to study their way, but they have too wide a gap in salaries. We settled on a scale with an upper limit of six hundred yuan and lower limit of sixty, a gap of ten-to-one between the highest and lowest paid. Later on, we decided that was too high; now we have a high of four hundred and a low of seventy-five. I don't think the higher brackets will ever get a raise, but the lower brackets certainly will. Money is of almost no use in a socialist society."

He made the larger implications of these policies clear.

[1] But now the Chinese have announced the June 13, 1966, execution of a "counterrevolutionary" student who stabbed a visiting Malian journalist and the wife of an East German official. The Chinese said the young man's father was executed in 1953 for murdering six persons while a landlord. The executed son had been arrested in 1965, said the Chinese, but "was dealt with leniently at that time."

"China is a big collective society that needs a small-scale democracy. Otherwise the people's initiative is sapped. A revolutionary people cannot be a rubber stamp. The Party's duty is to provide a correct atmosphere in which people can argue, then let them go ahead and argue. We have political power. We can do a lot by decree, but you become stale if you do this too much. We are trying things out. For the mind of the people to become stagnant is the worst danger we face."

What are the limits of debate in this society? The "overthrow of socialism" is not discussable, Tang said. We gained the impression that, in addition, there is a tendency to allow discussion to flourish until a decision is made but to curtail it afterward until the decision has been demonstrated in practice to be mistaken. "When something is emerging we must argue about it. When it has emerged, criticism can become an obstruction." The vast majority of the people, said Tang, give the regime support; perhaps 2 percent, he claimed, "would like to overthrow us." Sometimes conflicts occur indirectly, or so it seemed from Tang's reference to a play written by the Deputy Mayor of Peking which said the Chinese should learn from the good practices of a controversial feudal official of the Ming dynasty. (The Deputy Mayor was among those removed from Party responsibilities and governmental office in Peking as part of a "sweeping reorganization" that eliminated a "revisionist" group active for several years.)

What of those persons in China who in former times were well-off from commercial activities or landholding? Their "reeducation" toward socialism continues, Tang said. Former factory owners now receive 5 percent profit annually from their old enterprises on a seven-year plan which was extended an additional three years. The future of the plan is being discussed now, Tang said, and it may be ended in the coming year.

To most Americans this revolutionary temperament will seem unnatural, the product of fanaticism and ideological rigidity. We cannot be sure from this distance about the extent to which their thinking is realistic, but we believe it may well be, and certainly it is in purpose different from what is supposed by most American opinion. When the Chinese say that they "follow the thought of Mao Tse-tung in all things," we came to understand they were emphasizing one thesis in particular: that the Chinese people can master existence through their own resources and will power. The Marxist "relations of production" are often more important than the "forces of production" or, as Tang stressed to us, the Chinese depend primarily on the morale and energy of their people rather than the machine. What sounds like hero worship or the "cult of the individual" is the Chinese way to analyze development. Some practical examples of what is meant include:[2]

1. Workers building high walls and irrigation channels to prevent drought, by applying this concept: "A bad thing cannot automatically change into a good thing. Such a transformation demands a certain condition. What is it? It is the firm resolve to fight against natural calamities. Without that resolve bad things cannot be turned into good things. To turn bad things into good things we cadres and commune members must have the revolutionary drive shown by the 'Foolish Old Man Who Moved Mountains.' "

2. Making a clock to measure the frequency of an electric current. These workers had only an American clock to study which was too worn-down for their purposes. Certain workers wanted to copy other clocks made by "foreign authorities," but none of their models was precise enough. Finally, one of them found a new way to put together the needed clock,

[2] These examples are taken from the *Peking Review*, June 17, 1966.

though it required his intense research and experimenting under conditions of terrible heat and frustration. He relied on himself and on Mao's *On Practise*.

3. A labor group raising farm production and wanting to taper off. The cadres "carried on education in the need for uninterrupted revolution, and criticised the idea that there was no room for the further growth of production." They discovered new methods of sowing which led to increases. "There is no end to the revolution and there is no ceiling to production."

It is this incredible commitment, to enjoy revolutionary construction but not to relax with the benefits it brings, that perhaps accounts for the changes made in China since 1950. When one understands that Chinese civilization already has invented paper, silk, gunpowder, cannons, and compasses, when one understands that a Chinese official of long ago is remembered for telling the British that "we do not have the slightest need of your country's manufactures," one should then at least pause before doubting the realism of these "fanatics."

III

There are crucial international reasons, we found, for Tang's preoccupation with continuing this stoic revolutionary life within China. China's future as an effective and growing country is dependent, in the Chinese view, on ridding the world of imperial aggression and profit-taking on the part of the Western powers, and in particular the United States. Therefore, the Chinese reason, they must throw their weight behind any struggle being waged, from Vietnam to Santo Domingo, against the might of the U.S.

There are reasons for this attitude rooted in the Chinese

historical experience. Our trip through the Chinese Museum of
the Revolution helped us to understand the importance of the
long series of massacres and persecutions preceding the Chinese Communist victory. Their Revolution, it should be noted,
extended over twenty-five years of fighting; the only revolutionary conflict of similar length is the one in Vietnam. During
their struggle the Chinese endured every form of torture and
betrayal which colonial powers could summon; in addition, the
Chinese were to experience brush-offs by their powerful
Soviet neighbors, who placed the Russian national interest
ahead of the need of Mao and his followers. As the Chinese
view events from their experience, they believe that suffering
will accelerate unless the foreign intervention is ended deci-
sively. It perhaps was this experience that led Vice-Premier
Chen Yi to say in 1965 that unless the Vietnam question is
settled on the basis of self-determination, "the sufferings of the
South Vietnamese people would be prolonged under U.S.
imperialist domination and their sacrifices would be heavier
than they would sustain in their resistance."[3] We would hear
this theme stressed not only by Tang but by some of the
North Vietnamese and N.L.F. representatives we were to
interview; for example, Nguyen Minh Vy, of the North
Vietnam Peace Committee, told us that for the Vietnamese
"independence means the chance for existence."

"We ask ourselves," Tang said, "why are all the rich countries against us? Should a poor country such as China give
much foreign aid? And we answer: 'We are Communists and
belong with the weak, oppressed, and poor. If the rich like us,
something is wrong. We can only be free when all are free.' "

China therefore supports the Vietnamese, he said, adding a
gibe at the Soviets: "When we say support, we mean support."

[3] *Peking Review*, June 4, 1965.

It is no longer merely a special war in Vietnam, Tang believed, but one in which a grimmer future is being prepared. The American plan, as envisaged by Tang, is, first, the introduction of more troops into Vietnam; second, greater bombing; third, stationing soldiers along the Ho Chi Minh Trail, thus involving troops from Thailand and sealing off the Cambodian-Vietnamese border; fourth, expanded bombing of the Laotian Liberation Front forces; and finally, an attack on China.

"Our determination to help the Vietnamese won't be deterred by the threat of bombing China. We already expect that. They tell us: behave or we will bomb you. This really means there are two choices. First, to capitulate. Second, to say to them, 'Go ahead and bomb all you want; come in, destroy all the pots and pans, cups and saucers, the factories, Peking itself. We still will fight you.'" The phrase about "pots and pans" was borrowed from an expression used by Mao in the most depressing years during the Revolution, and it again reminded us of the historical framework through which the Chinese view the world.

Staughton observed that not only pots and pans but also little children would be destroyed by an American attack. "We can't help it," Tang replied straightforwardly. He said China was in some ways ready because of its early stage of growth: "We are only sixteen years old. From 1949 to 1952 we didn't build anything. Then [Nikita] Khrushchev withdrew his engineers, and it took time to recover. We have been building only ten years, really."

Did he think there would be a world war? we asked. He replied No, saying the war would take place in China. "Yes, I think they'll use nuclear weapons. Will the Soviet Union come to our aid? Not necessarily, I don't think so. But even with nuclear weapons they must send in troops to occupy. China is large enough," he said, laughing, "to accommodate five million

American troops, and once they get in they will never get out. Or"—he laughed harder—"they will use so many nuclear bombs on China that they will poison themselves."

He said China is prepared for annihilation: "China, after all, is not the only country in the world, and there will come along others to oppose U.S. imperialism." But he thought that alternatives to this grim future were more likely: "The use of nuclear weapons is a political question, one which the American Government cannot settle easily. It could lead to total moral and political isolation, even from the American people."

Thus we were led to talk about his perceptions of American society. The peace movement, he thought, is historically important. "After the November 27 Washington demonstration, I told Anna Louise [Anna Louise Strong, an American journalist living in China for many years], there is hope."

The Chinese seem to be shifting toward this confident view. A headline in *Peking Review* for February 11, 1966, read: "American People Say No to U.S. Imperialism." Chinese authorities are quoted in the article as calling the anti-war movement "a new awakening . . . unprecedented in scale." A February 7, 1966, article by "Commentator" in the paper *Renmin Ribao* said the peace movement will continue to grow and deepen even if attacked. The movement, said another Chinese source, has "pierced the long years of darkness in the United States."

These feelings perhaps accounted for the great interest and cordiality of our Chinese hosts. Tang's view was of particular interest since he had been for some years a resident of the United States. He offered a distinction between the Japanese-German militarism of the forties and the American intervention of the sixties which suggested his basis for hope.

"The Japanese and Germans first had to poison the minds of their people" before they could go to war, he said, but "since

Wilson's time the American reactionaries have had to defend their wars as if they were for democracy and peace." He added: "But this is just too clumsy for all Americans to believe. Johnson underestimates the decency and intelligence of the Americans. They can be a great people; I know, I lived there. What are the Americans going to say to their children if this war goes on and on?"

But, he granted, "even if worst comes to worst" and the war is escalated to China, "your movement will have failed, but we are prepared to suffer more." Returning to earlier themes, he said: "The Chinese people oppose war but are not afraid of it. I remember my childhood and the great oppression here. We would demonstrate, but protest was crushed immediately, and people were massacred. The worst thing that can happen is not to fight. More people get killed if you don't fight than if you do."

Isn't this more suffering than can be asked of a people, Staughton inquired. "Our people are used to getting tortured, killed, and so our people are disciplined. We have an old saying, 'When a country suffers, it has a future.' You will suffer terribly in your country, which is the heart of imperialism, before it changes. When the imperialists are driven back to Fortress America, then they will really crack down—you will suffer, you are not hard-boiled like ourselves. Yours is a violent country. When your standard of living drops because your colonies are gone, I pity you."

Almost inevitably we circled back to the problem of China's new generation and its differences from the old one. The importance of Vietnam in relation to this problem was summed up in one statement by Tang: "If Johnson escalates the war, he will save China from revisionism." This, too, was said with a laugh, but the basic point was serious: how can we show our young people that what we faced still exists today?

"I have asked myself, how can we invite Chiang Kai-shek back from Taiwan to show our young people. Now we don't need to—we have Johnson to show them instead."

We saw the truth of his statement confirmed in his own family the day he brought his two daughters, aged eleven and twenty-two years, to lunch with us. It was the only time that we were invited to share family life on our trip. The daughters both looked young for their ages, and both were charming. The eleven-year-old was a bit more lively than her sister, but the latter was interesting to us because she had been born in New York City. When we asked her if students were being prepared for a coming war with the U.S., she replied in her American-accented English: "The main thing is to study well, keep fit, and be ready." She smiled and added that many students were studying English. "If the U.S. enlarges the war, we will be interpreters. We will be the strong rear and, if called, we will even go to Vietnam and fight," she said.

The younger girl told us with striking poise that children her age "absolutely support the people in Vietnam." There are meetings and discussions at school, she said, and her class wrote a letter of support to Vietnam.

We were told that the older girl, who said she was learning "not to fear hardship and not to fear death," was teased by her friends for being from the United States and for holding the view that "there are some good Americans." If this seems to indicate bitterness in the Chinese, let it be said that we were received with the utmost friendliness by this family, and that this family, with the constant banter and discussion between father and daughters, seemed as free and wholesome as any we know in America. Once the younger girl told her father that he was cutting her off and, instead of reddening, he laughed, turned to us, and said, "We even practice criticism and unity in our families."

Some of this discussion was difficult for Herbert since his

Party group is at great odds with the Chinese on doctrinal matters. Nevertheless, he sat with silent courtesy and interest through the long talk. There were two exchanges between Herbert and Tang, however, which revealed something of the underlying controversy. Late in the discussion, when Tang was cataloging a number of foreign policy views different from those of the Soviet Union, Herbert, finally exasperated, said there was a contradiction between the Chinese willingness to see nuclear weapons spread and their opposition to nuclear armament for Germany. Tang said: "We will not engage in polemics. We know very well of your views." He spoke with a smile, but his words revealed the tremendous space between the two major Communist viewpoints and the difficulty of moderating or resolving the debate.

The other exchange came when Herbert talked of young American activists whose impatience, he feared, could lead to despairing and defeatist views of the world—a description that Herbert equally might offer of the Chinese revolutionaries. Tang's answer was significant, for it probably expressed his thoughts about China as well as youth: "But their impatience can create courage. And don't young people have the right to dream?"

He referred us to Steinbeck. "Do you remember that old book of Steinbeck's where the lady says, 'You can't kill us'? That is true. All the dictators from Genghis Khan down have failed. When I was a young man, we asked ourselves: how can we save China from being destroyed? Some young men got rich. We laughed at them, they were not to imitate. People with any sense joined us. Those with courage became Communists. Those who were a little afraid became sympathizers. Domestically, Chiang's policies helped us grow. The Japanese invasion certainly helped. It forced people to join. I went to visit a reservoir building project in 1952 and talked with a young woman who said she joined to fight the Japanese who had killed her family. There was no other way out for people. We have had three teachers: Chiang, Japan, and now Johnson. They teach our people a good lesson. Even their insults are helpful. We print them up for people to read. We have even printed John Foster Dulles' writings here."

One of the reasons he was pessimistic about an end to escalation in Vietnam was his theory that "war has its own laws of development" which have to be taken into account. Even the most reasonable persons in the "U.S. ruling circles," he said, cannot necessarily stop war after a certain point. As examples, he said Hitler did not have to invade Russia nor did Japan have to raid Pearl Harbor at the times they chose, but that war logic made events occur. Thus the U.S. could lose face, sink to a new low in the eyes of the world's people, lose leadership of the West, and still go on with the war. The danger, he said, is that "they don't understand oppressed peoples." He added: "They thought that by bombing North Vietnam they could force Hanoi to sell out. But this is just not what happens. The bombing of Hanoi or Haiphong seems pretty close now, but they are not capitulating."

"They make the further mistake of thinking we dominate the Vietnamese," he pointed out. "They used to say the Soviets dominated the Chinese, but they can't say that today. Nevertheless, they now give us too much credit for all this. This is because they do not understand a people's war."

"Because of your action, you help us carry out internationalist education," he said as we were about to leave for Hanoi. "We must tell people there are some good Americans. So much injustice has been done our people that it is easy to go overboard. They say there are two Chinas; well, we say there are two Americas, one of the monopolists and one of the people. If you could only stay and visit some schools. It would stick in the heads of the children."

4

IN HANOI I:
THE PEOPLE

I

On the plane to Hanoi, Staughton wrote: "Tuesday, December 28. We are in the tenth day of our trip and today, it seems, we will finally reach Hanoi. Last night was spent in Wuhan, an industrial city on the Yangtze, in company with a Chinese girl and a dozen Russians who are our fellow travelers on the Peking to Hanoi flight. I shared a hotel room with Ilya, a lyric poet from Novosibirsk, who at thirty has just published his fifth volume of verse in an edition of thirty thousand copies and who warned me against 'vulgarization' (his English was better than my Russian) of the theory of socialist realism.

"This morning we were awakened at five and at five-thirty shared with the Russians a Western breakfast of fried eggs, toast, and coffee. Besides Ilya, their party includes a senior economic adviser, two or three younger men, and a large number of women who sang vigorously as the bus took its load of Russians and Americans to a Chinese airport for the flight to Vietnam.

"From the airport bus, one saw the city beginning to stir to life, braziers glowing like red flowers in the open shop doorways, red and white Czech buses carrying workmen to their factories."

Later, he noted: "Our plane, a two-engine Soviet Ilyushin, has almost reached the North Vietnam border. The landscape below has shown almost as much variety as Chinese physiognomy: in north China, huge plowed fields of dun-colored loessial soil surrounding nucleated villages; in south China, smaller hamlets scattered through a checkerboard of rice paddies with the misty mountains of Oriental paintings as a backdrop."

We arrived in the early afternoon. Little girls dressed in colorful uniforms approached us hesitantly, with flowers and salutes.

Tom later summed up his first impressions in a speech on the March 25 and 26 International Days of Protest: "We were told by North Vietnamese and N.L.F. representatives in Moscow that life in Vietnam was calm and developing. But their words could not prepare us for the surprisingly peaceful atmosphere we found there, in the country where the Air Force has dropped more tons of destruction than during the whole Korean War. Perhaps the deepest impression we received in this war-torn place was that of a people who somehow manage to practice a rich life in the center of violence.

"Even before arriving in Hanoi we were struck by the grace, variety, and established identity of the Vietnamese, from Hanoi or the N.L.F., who met us along the Prague, Moscow, and Peking route. Our impression of an effectively organized society, with its own genuine character, was deepened as we flew low over the Chinese border into Vietnam.

Below rolled miles of delicately manicured fields, interrupted by areas of dense vegetation, a countryside developed with obvious care by generations of people. As we drove into Hanoi from the city's airport (too small to receive jets), the fields on both sides of the road were tended by people working actively in the huge paddies. If they were the quaking targets of the U.S. Air Force, it did not show in their appearance. In fact, if anyone was feeling an emotional shock it was ourselves as we entered this little world forbidden to Americans, so unknown to our people and so exposed to our military power.

"Hanoi itself, though fully prepared for battle, did not appear agitated or mobilized so much as it seemed to be enjoying the fruits of peace. Only an occasional soldier was visible, and infrequently a truck full of armed men or supplies would rumble down the pavement.

"The little lake in the center of Hanoi is ringed by cement-and-dirt bomb shelters where in the past flower gardens have bloomed. Most of the city's children are evacuated to safer provinces where they can continue school. But those remaining can be seen at play in the sand atop the shelters, running and shouting inside of them, and sometimes finding a convenient natural toilet behind them. Young couples spend evenings together on the park benches between the shelters, strolling along the rim of the lake, or riding bicycles together down the bordering lanes. Still others drink coffee or beer on the porch of an outdoor restaurant overlooking the lake, which under French rule was barred to Vietnamese.

"The theaters show numerous films and dramas about the war and its heroes, and people come in throngs to the shows each night. The war, however, cannot fully militarize art. In the streets of Hanoi, and on the radios there as well, we constantly heard poetry and music of all kinds. It is virtually the dominant sound, accompanied by the clicking of bicycle chains, women's wooden heels, and the soft chatter of voices, interrupted by occasional honks or the rattle of a two-car trolley.

"It could be said that such patterns are escapist. As we felt the atmosphere of Hanoi, we recalled the studies of 'irrational normality' of Europeans being bombed for the first time in World War II. But it seemed to us that the Vietnamese do not avoid the fact of American attack: too many of them wear rifles as they farm. Rather, they are so conditioned to war— since 1940, against Japanese, French, and Americans—that it no longer takes priority over civilian life. There is no national emergency which can fully erase the fact that shopping must be done, the fields tended, and young couples married."

II

The dozen or so Vietnamese who met us at the airport included several whom we would come to know well. Among them was Do Xuan Oanh, permanent secretary of the North Vietnam Peace Committee, and our principal interpreter. We all agreed that Do Xuan Oanh was not only a superb companion but also a mirror of the Vietnamese revolution: immediate and historical, clear and mysteriously complex, gentle and determined, ironic and sentimental. Oanh at first glance seemed young, cheerful, and somehow graciously prepared for our naïveté. As we grew to know him, our misconceptions fell one by one. He was forty-three, not thirty as we had guessed. He was of working class origin, not an urban intellectual. He was a man of great breadth, not simply the "American expert" on the Peace Committee. Like other Vietnamese we met, Oanh was reluctant to talk about himself; but as we accompanied

him from one event to another, bits of information emerged
about an astounding life. Oanh was born aboard a fishing boat
in Halong Bay along the eastern coast of North Vietnam, an
area known for the magical beauty of its thousands of coral
islands, now subject to Air Force blasting. Oanh claimed to
know every channel and every rock of that wonderland, and it
stands in his memory as a symbol of the fundamentally aes-
thetic nature of Vietnam. As a young man, he came inland
with a stepfather with whom he worked in the rich coal mines
owned by the French. His hard occupation did not kill an
interest in music which had developed in the coral islands, and
in the few hours available the young coal miner studied,
composed, and played the piano. His career changed again
with the development of national Resistance against the
French; he joined the Vietminh Army and lived in the jungle.
It was a new environment for the fisher's son turned miner,
but Oanh adapted well, even learning to make his cigars from
forest leaves. When he was assigned to guard French prisoners
of war, he began to learn their language in late night sessions.
Becoming fluent, he went on to master English as well. After
1954 his talents as an interpreter and writer led him to work
for the Peace Committee, while continuing to compose music.
"I am not an intellectual," he told us with pride. However, his
music and poetry are widely known. For instance, Oanh's song
"Emily," for Norman Morrison's daughter, was printed on
page 1 of the country's leading newspaper and is known and
sung throughout the country. He is shy about it, but sang it
for us on the occasion of a New Year's party arranged by our
hosts to "keep you company while you are away from your
families on this important day."

That evening we had the eerie experience of listening to the
Voice of America playing Bob Dylan's protest song, "Blowin'
in the Wind." We were told that the American program

explains to the Vietnamese how they are losing the war. With the American broadcast in the background, Oanh, who said, "I sing very bad," sang to us his song about Norman Morrison. The words of the song were translated in this rough way by Oanh:

Though in life he still has many people close to him,
Although his future would have been happy,
Why Morrison has not regretted his person and
He has sacrificed all his life of spring, his young life?
The flame which burned you will clear—enlighten—life,
And many young generations of people will again find the
*   horizon.*
Then a day will come when the American people will rise, one
*   after another, for life.*

How heroic is the flame of Morrison! The flame which burned
*   you*
Is shouting the shout of anger—that flame will be
Like an aureole—brilliant aureole—and it will burn the
Hearts of thousands and millions.
From this faraway land the flame of Morrison together with
*   Vietnam*
Opposes a common enemy.
Live—and people will remember your name as they remember
*   the*
Name of Troi in this land.
That glorious name for thousands of years later will still be
*   alive.*

Professor Thong, another of our hosts from the Peace Committee, softly told us, "In cultural performances, there is always a song about Morrison. Last night there was a great song about Morrison at the reception given by the Prime Minister for the New Year."

Oanh added, "One thing, the Vietnamese people consider Norman Morrison as a national hero. They put the name of Morrison together with Nguyen Van Troi."

We taught them how to make a human circle and sing "We Shall Overcome."

On New Year's during a stroll around one of Hanoi's lakes, Oanh told the legend of this "Lake of the Restored Sword." In the fifteenth century, he said, a national hero successfully resisted the Chinese after ten years of struggle. Afterward, while the hero was fishing, a turtle appeared in the lake, and asked that he return his sword to history. The turtle took the sword in his mouth and disappeared: "That means war is ended, peace restored."

"The family is our people's highest value," Oanh told us late one evening. He is the father of two children and a man whose own marriage has been deeply affected by the illness of his wife who, he said politely, "has not always been well since the French tortured her." He gave us insight on typical family "problems" when he talked laughingly about his own tendency, contrary to that of his wife, to impose discipline on the children to keep them from, for example, injuring his piano. His fatherly impatience seemed altogether "Western" to us as we listened.

Knowing Oanh gave us an intimate view of Vietnamese culture and social life. His nationalism was individualist and passionate. As we walked along the lake one evening, he began to talk about Vietnamese culture. The language, he reminded us, is such a poetic language that common dialogue becomes verse. It is a delicate and precious language, he said with great pride, "much harder to learn than Chinese." This culture, we came to understand, is yearning to be liberated from years and years of obscurity caused by the dominance of larger powers.

Watching Oanh work gave us insight about Vietnamese politics as well. We gained the distinct impression that there are a variety of separate and independent organizations. In order to move us from interview to interview, Oanh had to seek permission from the individual groups involved, and often we waited long hours for answers. This was caused not so much by "inefficiency" in the "totalitarian" structure, but by genuine autonomy of each among the proliferation of organizations. There were several occasions when we received the impression that we might have a short meeting with Ho Chi Minh; schedules and messages kept changing, but in the end there was no chance to meet Ho who was said to be still in the country. Another example of the process involved our request to visit some American prisoners; Oanh and the Peace Committee tried for days before receiving Army approval, and even then the meeting was held with only one American. Throughout it all, Oanh showed no sign of strain but kept on coordinating, improvising, replotting schedules, contacting officials, talking with us over meals about the possible ways we could use our remaining time. In his view this work was part of democracy: "We think democracy is best when there are many organizations." But he was not advocating a world of red tape: "We are a small country and do not have the Chinese problem of bureaucracy."

Oanh had been to Cuba, Moscow, Helsinki. This undoubtedly contributed to his appearance as a "man of this century," the description the Vietnamese give of Norman Morrison. But even his internationalism was deeply Vietnamese. One night after dinner, Staughton asked Oanh what he thought of the proposition that socialism, as an economic arrangement, was inevitable, but whether or not socialism would be humane depended on personal intent and action. As Oanh vigorously nodded his agreement, we felt that a genuine common ground had been found. We knew, too, what the Vietnamese contribution to a humane socialism would be; it was evident in the unembarrassed handclasps among men, the poetry and song at the center of man-woman relationships, the freedom to weep practiced by everyone—from guerrillas to generals, peasants to factory managers—as the Vietnamese speak of their country. Oanh put it in words quite simply; again and again, he said, "We Vietnamese are a very sentimental people." Here we began to understand the possibilities for a socialism of the heart.[1]

III

There were two other interpreters who became close to us, a man and wife named Nguyen Trung Hieu and Tran Thi Chi. We knew them less well than Oanh but well enough to catch some significant feelings.

Hieu was our cheerful second interpreter, somewhat less experienced than Oanh, and a good representative of the competent personnel known to anti-Communists as "apparatchiks." Hieu looked as young or younger than Oanh, but proved to be in his mid-thirties. He, too, had had military experience in the Resistance, and some formal education, though we discovered little about the details of his background.

One night walking back to the hotel we discussed the Communist Party. When Tom asked Hieu if he was a member, he said, with a poignant shrug, "No, just a staff member of the Peace Committee."

Finding him interested in the subject, we sat down at the

[1] Staughton met Do Xuan Oanh again at a peace conference in Geneva just before the bombing of Hanoi and Haiphong. Oanh spoke of the "great suffering" and "great optimism" of the North Vietnamese people. He said that his sister worked in a factory near Haiphong that had been bombed two days before Oanh left Hanoi for Geneva. He had not been able to determine if she was alive or dead, was expecting a cable when he reached Moscow on his way back to Hanoi, and in the meantime was attempting to keep calm. But Oanh added that the spring of 1966 meeting of the North Vietnamese National Assembly had been "more joyful than any I can remember since 1945."

hotel and listened to a frank, concrete, and "loyalist" set of opinions about the Party. We had wondered if competent people not chosen for Party membership might feel resentment toward their "Establishment," but when we questioned Hieu, his answer was negative. "The party is regarded by the people as an example. To be a member you are chosen by your associates who feel that you excel most among them at what you are doing together."

Thus, we were told, Party members in a factory are those whose work and attitudes set a pace for others; Party members in the Army are expected to take the greatest risks; Party members who teach or study are expected to win the intellectual respect of their colleagues. Hieu said he aspired to become a Communist, but suggested that it would require much more training and study on his part. His being "outside" the Party did not seem to rankle, perhaps not only because he accepts his limits but also because his own work is productive and satisfying.

Hieu, too, was building experience in international circles. Not as widely traveled as Oanh, he, nevertheless, had been to Moscow and Helsinki in the past year. Like Oanh he argued that Communism must have its own national character: "The Vietnamese people will make their own government." So intense was his nationalism that Tom asked, thinking of the Chinese-Soviet debate, "Suppose, Hieu, that this war ends and Vietnam is stabilized; then a revolution breaks out in India and the Liberation Front there calls for your aid while the American-supported Indians warn you either to stay out or be bombed. Would your nationalism make you identify with the revolution or keep you back from the conflict?"

Hieu said he did not know how to answer. "We will worry about that when the time arrives," he said.

The overwhelming impression we received from Hieu, however, was one of straightforwardness, dedication, and good-natured interest in whatever came. He recalled with great glee his night of folk singing in Moscow with members of the U.S. student movement. "We were up very late until four in the morning, and some of them had too much to drink," he laughingly explained. On the way to the country, we sang more songs for him: "We Shall Overcome" is his favorite, because of its "meaning and simplicity." We were surprised to discover that another favorite of his was "San Francisco," a hit in the Saigon of Hieu's childhood just as in the New York of Staughton's. But on reflection it seemed clear that Hieu would love the city of San Francisco.

Hieu slept little during our visit, and then often on a bunk provided him by the hotel. When he was not guiding us, he typed translations of material for us, arranged transportation, and, in general, exhausted himself to make our trip productive and comfortable. "Thinking and speaking in English so much is very tiring," he once said, the only time he admitted strain.

As we were packing on January 6, he discovered that Staughton's set of the *Selected Works of Ho Chi Minh* lacked two volumes; he rushed off to get his own copies. And early the morning of our departure, when we all had hugged good-bye, Hieu said from great depth that we were friends, and that we would see each other again in a freer world. The strength of the emotion, as always, left us dazed.

Chi was Hieu's wife. Taller and more slender than other women we met, she was a shy soul, with a beautifully featured face. We were introduced at a dinner held for us in the hotel the first night of our stay. Oanh and Hieu appeared with Chi, the three to sit at various corners of the table to interpret. Chi sat next to Tom. One of the first things she said was that it was her initial attempt to translate for an American. Her apology seemed irrelevant as her English was good, even though she nearly trembled from nervousness when she spoke.

As Chi gained confidence, she occasionally would talk about

herself and her people. She admitted once to Tom that she had expected American men to be "big and fast-talking" but was surprised, even embarrassed, to encounter respect and interest. She reminded us of the long history of cruelty toward women in many parts of Asia, and talked with considerable pride of the fact that women in her society today can choose their own husbands. This was one of the clear clues we received about the status of women in Vietnam. So crucial is the problem that the tenth and final point of the Vietnamese Communist Party's 1930 founding statement calls for "equality between man and woman." We would learn that since 1945 thousands of women have become intellectuals, engineers, and other professionals; that women make up about 15 percent of the membership of the National Assembly. Three days before our return we attended our first conference of Vietnamese intellectuals. A young girl, a student leader, said that three hundred thousand persons have had access to higher education since the revolution: "To you this may just seem a figure, but it means three hundred thousand lives with new wings." Emancipation is not necessarily complete, but Chi's tense willingness to step into an equal role helped us to understand the depth of this change.

Perhaps the most important communication we received from Chi, an unspoken communication we received at hundreds of points from dozens of people during our stay, was this: there were possibilities of the beginnings of dialogue among people a world apart. On our last night in Hanoi, Chi attended a farewell banquet held for us. At four the next morning she returned with others to accompany us to the airport. She said she did not feel well because her excitement about our visit and her tension at our leaving had prevented her from sleeping at all. Should we not begin to know such people?

Subversive
act of humanizing
enemy

IV

On our first afternoon in Hanoi, we were taken to the Museum of the Revolution. As we approached the small French-style yellow brick building, with surrounding tropical gardens and trees, we thought of our trip to the Chinese Museum. Located in the heart of Peking, on one side of a giant plaza, its pillars rising hundreds of feet into the air, it inspired awe by its size and the impression of power that it conveyed. The tall ceilings, spacious rooms, huge flags, and statues within the museum added to the effect. But if the physical plants of the two museums reflect the different appearances of the two countries, the historical records of the revolutions point to crucial similarities. Both were longer than any other socialist revolutions. The pictures and statues in both museums speak with silent eloquence of the countless martyrs and victims, old and young, men and women, workers and intellectuals, whose blood was spilled in the long struggles. In both museums are reminders of the ingenuity of the revolutionaries: in China, American weapons captured from Chiang Kai-shek; in Hanoi, a massive French cannon dragged away after Dienbienphu. In both, the heroes—Mao and Ho—are depicted in paintings and displays as teachers, not as symbols of violence.

Ho Chi Minh wrote in 1924 that his people were "crushed by the blessings of French protection," and hard times have not changed. Over tea, the museum's director cataloged the tortures used against revolutionaries. He himself had spent time in some of the prisons still used by the Saigon regime. Speaking of the island prison of Poulo Condor, known to Vietnamese in the same way that Parchman Penitentiary is known to Mississippi Negroes, he said that between 1957 and 1963 over one thousand South Vietnamese were held there.

Some escaped "without clothes"; the rest are gone. The torture, he said, is worse than under the French. "In a small cell, the French used to hold one to several persons. But now sometimes one hundred are kept in these cells. The only cool air comes from a small hole. People die little by little each day. The head of the jail comes and tortures the prisoners there. If the prisoners do not disclose anything, they are tortured the whole day. Sometimes they are made to stand naked under the sunlight. Sometimes they are put in a special cell called the tiger's cage."

As we prepared to leave, the director presented a gift: a little bronze arrow, which he said was thought to be perhaps one thousand years old, a reminder of the long Vietnamese tradition of battle against invading armies. We thanked him for the history of Vietnam. His associate, who had admitted with shyness that his part in history included having fought at Dienbienphu, did not attempt to stop weeping as we left for our first meetings with those who make history today.

Our contacts with "ordinary Vietnamese citizens" also occurred during visits to two factories, one in Hanoi, the other in the provincial city of Namdinh, and to an agricultural cooperative. These visits were carefully arranged by our hosts, and we have no reason to believe that the enterprises we toured or the workers and peasants with whom we spoke were typical. Yet we were permitted to talk freely with anyone we chose, and when the Vietnamese learned that Tom's tape recorder gave them the opportunity to communicate directly with the people of the United States, they spoke with great eagerness. Our sense was of individuals unburdening their hearts rather than human robots explicating the Party line.

The factory in Hanoi manufactures agricultural implements. Row after row of heavy lathes and presses were noisily in use, and an enormous crate stenciled with Soviet labels and instructions was about to be opened. We walked past the usual shallow air-raid shelters to reach the entrance of the large shedlike building. The war was evident also in many large posters including one of Norman Morrison, captioned, "The flames of Morrison will never die," and in pictures of American protest demonstrations. There was excitement among the workers when Staughton pointed to a picture of a demonstration in Berkeley on October 16, 1965, which showed a picture of Staughton speaking from the back of a pickup truck. We talked with the factory manager and about a dozen workers in a room adjoining the plant.

The manager was wearing a white shirt with tie, and a sports coat. "We like Americans," he said, "because of their practical minds. We like Americans because of the first declaration by Lincoln. Our own declaration takes phrases from Lincoln. We like the American people because of their industry and science. If there was no bombing and strafing, our factory might have developed quicker." Suddenly he broke down, and several of the workers became moist-eyed. "The word American means something beautiful to us, but it has been difficult to say since the intervention. Many of our workers regrouped from the South." As if to say something about his factory as well as to suggest his basis of hope, he said of Norman Morrison: "He sacrificed himself for justice, not for economic self-interest."

The factory was named for a king who fought Genghis Khan, and was built on the site of a former French prison. The manager talked about the failure of past conquerors, saying the Vietnamese will keep their independence "even if the whole economic basis of our life built in the last ten years is lost or destroyed." "During the Resistance," he said, "we ate only potatoes, maize, vegetables, and we will do it again."

Workers work a six-day week, eight hours per day, get ten

days' vacation each year. Living quarters are located two kilometers away, and it is up to the individual worker whether or not he wants to live there or at another home. The factory sponsors an art and culture club and a self-defense militia. Formerly, it maintained a rest house near the sea for the workers, "but it is impossible to go there now." The state pays for special diets for those who need them, and there is a free infirmary staffed by a doctor and two assistants. The youth of the factory gave a "Nguyen Van Troi plow" to a province which shot down U.S. aircraft.

While Staughton and Herbert toured the plant, Tom tape-recorded discussions with several workers. Again and again, their answer to the question, What difference has the revolution made in your life?, was education. One, whose son began fighting the French when he was ten years old, told us that he "followed his factory to the forest"—helping to transport it out of enemy range—thus "joining the Resistance by building." His children all go to school now. Another was studying in the evenings and soon would receive his engineering degree. A third said his father died of diseases brought on by over-work. Formerly, he could not have hoped for an education. In the factory as a whole, we were told, one hundred were studying at the university level and two hundred at the high school level.

One man told us, "Workers have the right to do anything they like—attend the university, study music. Our children will be the good builders of the country, and the future will be more splendid."

Perhaps their strongest reaction came, as it did with whom-ever we talked, when we asked their opinion of the American claim that Communism is tyranny. "What you have just said," one replied after hearing the Western view, "is quite different from reality." He added, "My children and family now are well off. In the old days if you wanted to go to school you had to labor very hard. Now all my children go to school."

Another said, "When I was fifteen I had to work as an apprentice without any pay. At present, as you may see for yourself, I have enough food and clothing and now we go to school. Life is still hard, but it is improved."

The commander of the factory's self-defense force, who formerly was an officer at Dienbienphu, gave "complete approval" to the idea of American working people visiting Vietnam to "discuss how to abolish poverty and the exploitation of man." He spoke for all of them when he assured us of the inevitable victory of his people. We still do not know if the factory was destroyed in the American bombing of the Hanoi area which began June 29.

Later, in the provincial city of Namdinh, Staughton was told by textile workers that they participated in management in two ways. First, there are production teams whose members discuss everything among themselves, then report through the head of the team to the manager. Second, every three months there is a congress of all plant workers and functionaries to which the manager reports. Resolutions adopted must be carried out by the manager.

These workers also described the election of model workers, who must be distinguished by their ability to produce well, study well, and help other workers.

In contrast to these "new Vietnamese men and women" is the image of corruption abroad and in the South which is widely held in Hanoi. Personnel in Hanoi of the International Control Commission, created by the Geneva Conference, were described to us as persons who do nothing, smuggle whiskey, use hair shampoo and Players cigarettes, and were called "milkmen" because they ride in white cars. Similarly, the other side showed us a film in which D.R.V. soldiers were portrayed as courageous gentle persuaders; but their opposite number in the "puppet Army" had long hair and sunglasses, his uniform was unkempt, he chased women and was indifferent to peasants. His chiefs were an old Catholic priest and simple-minded Americans. In the end, he was afflicted by a crisis of conscience and was won over when he saw how much the villagers enjoy life in a "liberated" village.

We also visited the Phu Dien cooperative not far from Hanoi. The chairman presented statistics which, if only half true, would amply explain why peasants as well as workers have reason to be thankful for the Communist revolution.

In this six-acre village of about 1,000 inhabitants, the chairman said, 137 persons starved to death in 1945 and 45 were killed during the French occupation. Thanks to land reform over two thousand plots of land have been consolidated into ninety-five. The chairman stated that 75 percent of the households in the village now have bicycles, boiled-water flasks, and mosquito nets, while 85 percent of the homes now are built of brick.

Bamboo poles were the only means of transport in the past. "Now we have liberated shoulders of eighty-five percent of the work. And fifty percent of the land is plowed by tractors," he said.

As everywhere in North Vietnam, the proudest claims center around education. Everyone was at school including the oldest.

But this also was a village at war. It had a small bomb shelter built in August, 1965, and, as one fighter told it, "from age sixteen to the old people, everyone has his own weapon." Tom talked for over an hour with two girls, both twenty years old, who were part of the thirty-seven-member guerrilla group which was organized in 1960. They had studied "people's war," and practiced shooting at "puppet targets." Besides this, they said, women, who now make up 70 percent of the village population, "insure everything for men" by going to the fields with rifles on their shoulders. Two nights each week they attend classes in history, literature, chemistry, and other subjects. They, too, became most emphatic when questioned about the nature of Communism: "We love our Party and we love socialism because thanks to our Party our country was liberated. That is why we do everything to protect the happy life we now have. That is why we do our best in production, in education, in fighting, and why we prepare carefully for the U.S. aircraft. . . . As we are women, we are conscious of our duty, that is why we do everything, not to follow orders from our Party or our Government or from China, but to do, by ourselves, by our consciousness, not relying on anyone."

When they have something to say to the Government, do they speak up? Tom asked. "Yes, of course, if you want to have something to say to our Government, say directly."

In the growing dusk, someone placed a small lantern on the table around which Tom and the villagers were gathered. Solemnly and with disarming simplicity the villagers began to question Tom. "Do the American people know that the Government is escalating the war to North Vietnam, and what do they think of the war in Vietnam, and do they know the reality of Vietnam?" "So what do you think when you visit our village, because your Government says we are not free and we live in slavery?"

Tom told them there possibly is no place in America where people feel "community" as much as in this Vietnamese village, and that, therefore, the American people, not knowing the "enemy," might support a long and terrible escalation.

The faces in the candlelight were somber and interested. The silence was broken by a bell summoning the people to school. As the chief bade Tom good-bye, he said: "We would like to say to you, on behalf of everyone, that we extend our thanks for your calling upon us, and we wish you to convey to the American people, especially laboring people, our best wishes, and also our best wishes to Mrs. Anne Morrison."

As we reflect back, neither of us ever will forget the teen-age girl in that village whose head hardly came to our shoulders, who seriously told us: "If the American planes come to my village, I will shoot them down." She meant it. Here is how the North Vietnamese officials brief their people on "bare-handed fighting" against strafing American Air Force jets:

How to shoot down an American plane with a rifle is simple. When an enemy plane comes diving toward you, there is a split-second moment when the plane's rudder and stabilizer become invisible and the whole plane looks like a big round dot. This is the only chance you have to shoot down the plane, and it is of course the most dangerous moment when you are exposed to the enemy attack. Don't shut your eyes. Pull the trigger.[2]

V

Most of our time was spent in the area of Hanoi, but one day we did set off toward the countryside to view the effects of our country's bombing. Our hosts told us to prepare for a two-day journey, but an air raid warning caused the trip to be canceled after less than a day.

Late one afternoon, two cars rolled up to our hotel, both heavily camouflaged with branches and leaves. As the sun set, we drove out of Hanoi on the highway south, through poor

[2] Quoted from a report by Minoru Omori, foreign editor of *Mainichi*, datelined Hanoi, September 25, 1965, *Viet-Report*, November–December, 1965, p. 7.

neighborhoods and past miles of still farmlands. This part of the road, and the train tracks paralleling it, had not been bombed yet; we doubt that they still remain intact. After about an hour's driving, we saw the first bomb damage as we detoured around a bridge not yet rebuilt.

As darkness came, we entered Namdinh, a city of perhaps ninety thousand persons in Nam Ha province about one hundred miles south of Hanoi. A famous textile area, it has a large Catholic population. Similar to medium-size Southern cities which rear up out of the countryside, Namdinh was alive by night. Small beams lighted the way for pedestrians, people on bicycles, and occasional drivers, as they went about their business. Shopping was done in dimly lighted stores, and people gathered along the streets in small knots to talk. Our car stopped at a one-story building where we shared a meal with representatives of the city and county organizations. They were patient as they discussed the numerous times that American planes have attacked their land. Then we were driven to a nursery school devastated by bombs and rockets. By flashlight, we were read a slogan still legible on a broken wall: "Let Us Bring Up Healthy Children, Let Us Educate Good Children."

A woman told us, "When the U.S. aircraft bomb this place, the parents of the children were in the factory, and the children live in this kindergarten and nursery school. They were sleeping, upstairs and downstairs both, and the planes were bombing them at night, the same time as now."

Oanh said that minutes before the raid which destroyed the school, leaflets were dropped wishing good health to the children. Nearly the entire Western press has joined the North Vietnamese in saying the American pilots are striking civilian as well as military targets. But as we moved through the broken bricks under those dark skies, viewing the reality of war for the first time, it was difficult to believe that anything was real: the bombing, the school, the night, our own presence on such forbidden ground.

We also saw a bombed pagoda that night. We were told that it was hit on August 4, 1965, the bombs destroying part of the roof and numerous statues. "We heard an explosion, but we couldn't tell how many bombs were falling on the pagoda," a monk recalled.

We went, too, to that part of the textile factory which had not been removed yet to the forests. The machinery was worked by a team of women, their guns hung nearby, who paused only a moment to greet us before turning back with a coldness that made us wonder about their feelings. Outside we spent a few minutes talking with the small defense crew, alert by their small machine gun, watching the night sky.

Later we talked with a woman who worked in the factory: "When the first bomb fell, I was at production. I was in front of the weaving machine. As a young person, when the enemy came, I joined the fighting. I fought by the side of the factory in order to defend the factory. I don't want bombs falling near to us, by the side of our factory."

Our discussion was cut short by an interpreter who broke in to say, "In order to insure your safety, we propose that the interview stop here, and we hope to meet again." One of our country's planes was near the coast and, as a precaution, we were warned to depart. We said good-bye to about forty of our hosts, and drove by moonlight back to Hanoi. Feeling overprotected in comparison with the people left in Namdinh, Tom remarked to Hieu that the people seemed to be calm.

"They have no other way than to be calm," Hieu replied.

5

IN HANOI II:
THE SYSTEM

I

Our first few days in Vietnam were designed by our hosts to serve as an introduction to their society. We met leaders of youth groups, women's groups, non-Communist political parties, trade unions, Buddhist and Catholic religious organizations. Professor Thong, who also is director of the D.R.V. Pedagogic Institute, told us about Vietnamese history. Many of these persons assembled again on New Year's Day to ask us questions about the American peace movement, and once more at a banquet January 6 before we left.

The morning of December 28 we met with leaders of the Fatherland Front in its yellow stone building near downtown Hanoi. This organization is an extension of the Vietminh Front, formed in 1941, and the later Lien Viet Front, which served as the vehicles of the Ho Chi Minh–led revolution. Today it functions, alongside the Workers (Communist)

Party, the national Government, and the Army, as a major forum in which policy dialogue takes place in North Vietnam. It is the nearest parallel in North Vietnam to the South Vietnam National Liberation Front.

Present around the inevitable tea tables were members of the Peace Committee, our interpreters, a labor leader who also holds an official position corresponding to that of attorney general in the United States, the vice-chairman of the Women's Union who also is a member of the Fatherland Front Central Committee, the bonze (monk) who is president of the Buddhist Association, the vice-secretary-general of the Democratic Party, the secretary-general of the Fatherland Front, Professor Thong, a Catholic bishop, and a lawyer who heads the Socialist Party.

The bonze spoke first, saying: "There was much persecution of the Buddhists during the colonial days." After the revolution of 1945, he said that "some Buddhists hesitated to enter the Northern zone because of the charge that the D.R.V. was anti-Buddhist." He added: "But in fact the D.R.V. has a good policy. Many bonzes have been helped, many pagodas rebuilt. After Geneva, many Buddhists were kept in the South; they have had a hard life. The 1963 demonstrations and repressions convinced many Buddhists who were deceived before about Communism." He said there were active Buddhists in the Hanoi Government, that religious holidays were recognized by the D.R.V., that each village has a pagoda, that many intellectuals including the chairman of the Peace Committee "follow Buddhism."

The previous evening we had spoken in the hotel lobby for a few minutes with Le Dinh Tham, who is chairman of the Peace Committee, a doctor, and a leading Buddhist. "The Buddhist movement is a continuous one," he said. "Strong at some moments, not so strong at others. Especially the young

Buddhist students are active. From 1963 to 1965 they have been brutally repressed in the South, and perhaps because of that they are trying to find another method of struggle. Yes, the Saigon Government has Buddhists loyal to it; the only Buddhist office in Saigon is an instrument of the Government. Sometimes they send their people to visit Asian countries, but they represent only themselves. The Buddhist movement has its own representative within the N.L.F. Central Committee. A majority of the Buddhists are members of the N.L.F. or sympathizers."[1]

Hoang Quoc Viet (the "attorney general") broke in with several comments as the bonze finished his presentation. The most important was: "Every Vietnamese should have the charity of the Buddha."[2] Later, on New Year's Eve, Viet told

[1] Denis Warner presented one example of bonzes driven toward the National Liberation Front. In 1961, he reported, Diem's forces attacked innocent people in a part of the Mekong delta, saying that the villagers were in favor of the wanton shelling because it protected them. "The following month, after the army had retired, leaving thousands of unhappy peasants behind it, Buddhist bonzes petitioned the province chief in Tra Vinh against the shelling of hamlets and pagodas and to demand the release of their imprisoned fellows. Some months later their leader, Superior Bonze Son Vong, appeared on the lists of the central committee of the Viet Cong's National Liberation Front." (*The Last Confucian* [Baltimore, 1964], p. 153).

[2] Viet reappears several times in our narrative, and has an interesting background. Marvin Gettleman reprinted a political statement by Viet, "Johnson Swindle Will Certainly Fail," which appeared in *Nhan Dan*, April 21, 1965. Gettleman listed him as chairman for the Standing Committee of the International Conference for Solidarity with the Vietnamese People, Against U.S. Imperialist Aggression, and for the Defense of Peace. (*Vietnam*, pp. 419–425).

Bernard Fall commented:

He has no legal training whatever but was the leader of a Vietnamese Communist labor union since its creation on August 20, 1946. An old-line Communist who had spent five years in French jails, he took an early interest . . . in the DRVN's judicial system. In 1946, he wrote a now-famous circular addressed to the courts, chiding them for a too-literal application of the law; in his view, it was their duty to put "out of

us he had rushed back from the country to have dinner with us because they all thought it was sacrificing of us to be away from our families during the Christmas season, and because he had heard we felt "ill at ease" about the publicity in the U.S. On that occasion he reported that there had been no bombing for three days, but called it the "silence before the storm." He said the United States is knocking at many doors, but not the "accurate door." More sentimentally, he said of Morrison that the leading Vietnamese poet had cried while writing a poem in tribute. He and Oanh had cried also. He compared the poem to an old classic story in which "unity comes from shared sufferings."

Viet spoke with more authority than any other person with whom we became well acquainted on the trip. He was amusing, fatherly, polemic; but he had a greater tendency than any other Vietnamese we met to view events as he wanted them to be. For example, a trade unionist himself, he clearly exaggerated the opposition of American workers to the war; he thought the electrical workers caused the blackout of the Northeast in the autumn of 1965.

The next speaker was the elderly Catholic bishop, Ho Thant Bien. He told us that his religion was brought to Vietnam by

---

commission the enemies of the people, and not, by applying to the letter some obsolete text, to let them escape from just punishment of their crimes." (*The Two Viet-Nams* [New York and London, 1964], p. 146).

Joseph R. Starobin met Viet when he visited the Vietminh jungle headquarters in 1952 and characterized him as follows:

. . . one of the best known Communist leaders . . . a government minister, and also chairman of the Viet Nam's Confederation of Labor. He is a short, solid man with a thin mustache over tight, hard lips, and a large forehead under a dome of black hair: his young daughter of nine, born and reared in the forests, a girl with a buster-brown hair cut and a bashful smile, had been standing in the pathway as we arrived. (*Eyewitness in Indo-China* [New York, 1954], p. 119).

the French and Spaniards three hundred years ago. "Under the French, Vietnamese never were higher than the level of clergyman in the Church; no bishops, no promotions.[3] A majority of Catholics followed the revolution. Only the high-ranking ones followed the colonialists. The charge that Communism is against religion is aimed at separating the Catholic people from the national struggle." (The number of Catholics in North Vietnam is estimated to be eight hundred thousand; there are about two million Catholics in Vietnam as a whole.) We have a confused impression about the relations between the North Vietnamese Church and the Vatican, however. This gentleman said there were "normal relations." "Concerning theory, we follow any order from the Vatican. Concerning society, we follow our people," he told us. He said he himself was appointed and promoted by the Vatican. Professor Thong later would indicate that relations were more muddy than that.

Another Fatherland Front leader was Tran Dang Khoa, a man of perhaps fifty, distinguished and confident in appearance, concerned to tell us all he could. He had been an engineer, educated in France, helped to found the Democratic Party during the "struggle against Fascism" in 1944, and now represents "the progressive tendencies among the patriotic bourgeoisie and intellectuals and petite bourgeoisie." He is vice-chairman of the National Assembly. Telling us more of his history, Khoa said that first he had supported the Vietminh Front, became an affiliated member, joined the general insurrection in August, 1945; "then I joined the land reform revolution, built up people's power, helped to build socialism

[3] Other Vietnamese informants described segregated Catholic Masses under the French rule during which French soldiers stood at the church doors with guns to keep Vietnamese from entering. Professor Paul Mus, born in Vietnam and an authority on Vietnamese religion, told us this was true and added that in rural areas when a Vietnamese peasant met a French priest he often was expected to fall to his knees before speaking.

in the D.R.V. until 1954." There are a number of Democrats in the National Assembly and one is both secretary-general of the Party and minister of state farms. This man was formerly minister of water conservation, but since 1960 has held his post in the National Assembly. The strength of the Democrats lies in cities: Vinh, Hanoi, Haiphong. They have a "branch" in the South, created before the country was divided.[4]

Do Xuan Sang, a lawyer who is head of the Socialist Party, spoke next. The Socialist Party was formed in 1946 with "scientific socialism as the basis of its activities." Another visitor to Vietnam was told in 1952 that it "had been formed in 1946 from among that small body of Viet Nam intellectuals who had found their political home with the French Socialists but who were disillusioned when the Socialist leaders in Paris proved to be the most bitter foes of the Republic."[5] Today most of its members are intellectuals. They too participate in "the people's power"—the Government and National Assembly. The secretary-general of the Socialist Party is one of the vice-chairmen of the Assembly; another Socialist is minister of culture; and Socialists are active in the administrative councils of the cities. We would discuss these "parties of the bourgeoi-

---

[4] In 1952, Joseph R. Starobin (during a similar meeting with leaders of the Lien Viet Front at its jungle headquarters) heard a similar presentation from the then-leader of the Democratic Party, Duong Duc Hien. He wrote:

"Of course, we do not share the Marxist philosophy," he [Duong Duc Hien] said. "Our roots are in nationalism. It has taken us some time to realize that in a people's democracy such as a Free Viet Nam will be tomorrow, there will be room for a 'national bourgeois' class." He envisaged a real future for his class, but he admitted that the leadership of the country would necessarily be with the working class, and the Lao Dong Party. That had been the only force capable of resisting the imperialists and winning independence. (*Eyewitness in Indo-China*, p. 123).

[5] *Ibid.*, p. 123.

sie"—Socialists and Democrats—in greater detail with Professor Thong a little later.

Le Thi Xuyen of the Women's Union spoke next. A woman of perhaps forty, with a sweet face, wearing a blue shawl and dress with black sweater, she was very small in her big chair. Earnestly trying to communicate, she leaned out to the edge of the chair when speaking. "Most women had no rights and were illiterate under feudalism and colonialism. None of us were engineers, few women were intellectuals." During the Resistance, she said, both married and single women joined the militia—at factories and schools as well as in rural areas. "Vietnamese women have always been laboring people. Now the government lets thousands of women study mechanics. Women feel like the masters of production," she said. They practice "three responsibilities": 1. production; 2. home work, educating the children, looking after the old; 3. serving in the Army in first aid, liaison, and actual fighting. There are sixty-two women in the National Assembly, or 13 percent of the membership. Twenty-five percent of the members of the people's councils (the province governments) are women. They are directors and vice-directors of factories and co-ops. But this woman was not primarily a tabulator of numerical progress. She spoke some of the most touching words we heard. "Tell the American women," she said, "not to let the Government make their sons criminals" for burning their draft cards. "Anne Morrison is just like our own sisters and relatives. We have seen photos of her carrying her baby. We see that she is both mild and energetic. Please invite her to come." She wept when Staughton told her of his closeness to the Morrison family.

During this talk, Tom wrote the following notes: "Only every now and then you remember this place is being bombed and strafed every day. Perhaps because they have fought so long, they have learned how to build life even while in war. Production goes on, arts and music, poetry, romantic life, not during intervals between fighting but as the fabric out of which the struggle is maintained. If there was hysteria here, I don't know how cool I could be. As it is, their peacefulness spreads to me."

II

The next day we talked with Professor Thong, whom we had first met at the airport. Retiring, smiling, frequently wiping his glasses, he seemed at first a typical academic. Later in the revolutionary museum we saw a picture of the professor in jail with Nguyen Huu Tho, the Saigon lawyer who now is president of the N.L.F. Thong had been the president and Tho the vice-president of the Saigon Peace Committee. They were arrested together and, subsequently, escaped together. When we next encountered Professor Thong, we viewed him with new respect.

Our talk began with informal discussion of the Catholic bishop's statement that relations between the Vatican and the North Vietnamese Government were normal. Thong said relations were "abnormal" and that the bishop's appointment to a church post was being delayed.

His intention, however, was to survey Vietnamese history for us. What struck us most about his lengthy talk was its intense nationalism. Clearly this is no ordinary nationalism. Professor Bernard Fall noted that the history of the Vietnamese people is "almost unique" in the way the people have "succeeded in maintaining their national identity" during long periods of foreign intervention.

Thong said: "Our written language originated three hun-

dred years before Christ. Under French domination, we found
many relics of the past. Some historians said these belonged to
an earlier and different nationality. Since independence we
have continued research, and proved that these relics belong to
ancestors of the Vietnamese people. Among our evidence is
the bronze arrow. Up to now there has not been enough
evidence, but many clear signs that we have a very old culture
and history.

"In Vietnam at the present there are many ethnic nationalities, some with very close ties to the relics. Some still use tools
of this kind.

"The Vietnamese people came into existence 'on the spot,'
so to speak, but have mixed blood with the Indonesian and
Chinese people. There has been mixing of culture with India
and China, but ours is a distinctively Vietnamese culture.

"Chinese feudalists invaded Vietnam in the first century B.C.
Until the tenth century there was a dependent relationship
with China. Not the same as modern invasions; more like the
Roman Imperial Empire.

"When possible the Vietnamese put up their own government and administration, and retained their habits and
languages. There was an insurrection every century. Two particular ones are still remembered widely. One was in the first
century by the two Trung sisters. It was successful in setting
up a national government for a few years. The second was in
the sixth century, also successful, in which we had our own
national name for over fifty years.

"We achieved independence in the tenth century after a
great battle. We remained generally independent up until the
nineteenth century but often we were fighting the Chinese
feudal aggressors, for instance in the eleventh and twelfth centuries, and against the Mongol aggressors in the thirteenth. For
ten years in the fifteenth century we were dominated by the

Ming dynasty, and in the eighteenth century we had to repel another Chinese invasion.

"There was an important insurrection in the late eighteenth century. One of its aims was to unify the country. Down to the fifteenth and sixteenth centuries Vietnam extended south to Hue. 'Tonkin,' 'Annam,' and 'Cochin China' are all French names. 'Tonkin' is based on Chinese characters and means 'capital in the East.' 'Annam' was a term borrowed from the Chinese feudalists meaning 'pacified South.' It referred both to the central highland area and to all Vietnam. At the time of the insurrection Vietnam was divided into a Northern state and a Southern state, each controlled by a feudalist family.

"The revolution lasted thirty to forty years. Each family recognized that Vietnam was one country and each wanted to control it. The king was in North Vietnam. The family in the South wanted to liberate the North to 'protect' the king. The people insisted that Vietnam was one country. There were many peasant insurrections. The one at the end of the eighteenth century was successful, threw out both families, and unified the country. Its first slogan was: Support the king to unite the country. The king asked rescue from China, which sent troops. The king lost prestige. The remaining members of the king's family sought assistance from the French. In 1802 the Nguyen family of South Vietnam occupied the North and overthrew the leader of the peasant revolution.

"Besides nationalism the goals of the revolution were: one, the use of Vietnamese instead of Chinese script; two, educational examinations; three, military assistance from foreigners to build up a navy; four, permission for the people to study Western techniques.

"The revolution was led by Nguyen Hue, who when head of the state was called Quanh Trung. He came from a well-to-do peasant family, one of his two older brothers was a middle-ranking civil servant. His family lived in the North and was taken to the South by the Nguyen family when they over-threw the regime.

"The documents of the revolution were destroyed, its policies were unfulfilled. After the death of Nguyen Hue there were conflicts among his officers so that the people did not continue to support his dynasty. Nevertheless, the regime created by this eighteenth century revolution was the 'root of a new society.' "[6]

Professor Thong summarized the two thousand years of Vietnamese history prior to French occupation: "The most enduring thing was the national tradition of the people. We always have been fighting against aggressors. The country remained, and developed with its own particular characteristics."

We asked questions about this concept of nationhood. For instance, what about dependence on China? Thong responded: "The Vietnamese king, like the Chinese king, styled himself head of all human beings. In practice the Vietnamese king addressed the Chinese king as his superior. It was like the relation between the Holy Roman Emperor and the kings of Europe. In fact the Vietnamese were independent, but they did not want war with China. So they stayed formally within the Chinese system: defeated them when they invaded, but called them 'emperors.' "

[6] The Tay Son Rebellion (1772–89) was a complex revolt against the two warring dynasties, the Nguyen and the Trinh, which had ruled South and North Vietnam respectively. The rebellion was partly dynastic and partly a popular movement against tyranny. A young prince of the Nguyen family, Nguyen Anh, escaped from the rebels and finally with French help was able to overthrow them. Nguyen Anh took the name Gia Long, and established the unified state of Vietnam in 1802. See Roy Jumper and Marjorie Weiner Normand, "Vietnam: The Historical Background," *Vietnam*, ed. Gettleman, p. 16; Joseph Buttinger, *The Smaller Dragon: A Political History of Vietnam* (New York, 1958), pp. 175–176, 197, 233–242, 264–267; John F. Cady, *Southeast Asia: Its Historical Development* (New York, 1964), pp. 281–284.

Thinking of current realities, Staughton asked: "You were a free people, but you let the beaten foe save face?"

"Yes," Thong said, "that is a reality. We are a very practical people. In the fifteenth century we captured the general staff of the Ming dynasty and gave them boats to go home. Probably because of this tradition Ho said that if the United States withdrew, Vietnam would lay down a red carpet for it."

Herbert asked: "Have you ever invaded other countries?"

"Once in the twelfth century," the professor replied. "Also in the nineteenth century the Nguyen dynasty wanted to make Laos and Cambodia dependent on Vietnam. It did not send troops: it was a kind of neo-colonialism. But historically Laos, Cambodia, and Vietnam are three countries with different cultures. The Laotian language has the same origin as Vietnamese, but the Cambodian language is quite different."[7]

Still seeking to probe the meaning of nationalism for the professor, we asked about the historical position of minorities. Thong said there had been a "traditional unity." In the highland minority areas there was much land and few people, in the deltas just the reverse. "There was no racial discrimination. This is an inheritance from the French, who brought people from the South Vietnamese mountains to the cities for exhibition. In preparation for the August revolution [of 1945] most leaders lived in the minority areas in the mountains, from which many leaders came," he commented.

[7] In contrast to Professor Thong's account, Western scholars agree that on the eve of European colonization Vietnam was itself an expansionist power. After freeing itself from Chinese domination in A.D. 939, Vietnam expanded southward and westward into neighboring kingdoms until the seventeenth century. Bernard Fall commented that Vietnamese expansion at the expense of the Champa was "as thorough a job of genocide as any modern totalitarian state could have devised." (*The Two Viet-Nams*, pp. 12–19). See also Jumper and Normand, *Vietnam*, ed. Gettleman, pp. 14–15; Robbins Burling, *Hill Farms and Padi Fields: Life in Mainland Southeast Asia* (Englewood Cliffs, N.J., 1965), p. 106; Donald Lancaster, *The Emancipation of French Indochina* (London and New York and Toronto, 1961), pp. 15–17; Cady, *Southeast Asia*, pp. 103–106.

Professor Thong then spoke of the French occupation and the Vietnamese resistance. "From 1858 to 1883 the French invaded under the pretexts of, first, a treaty signed by the Nguyen dynasty, and second, mistreatment of Catholics. At first the people supported the king against the French, but when the royal family compromised, the people still fought. There were many heroes, some of them from feudal families. There were two kings who advocated resistance and were accordingly exiled. The people rebelled but had no ideal. A leader in the North was Hoang Hoa Tham, a peasant. He was assassinated in 1912 and his daughter taken to France. But she came back to Vietnam and still lives here today."

Using the same phrase we had heard in Peking, Professor Thong continued: "At the beginning of the century there was a search for the means of liberation. Some looked to Japan. Some, admiring France, proposed to follow the revolution of the democratic bourgeoisie. In 1908, France suppressed the study of French bourgeois ideology. Others advocated secret organization and armed struggle, such as Ho Chi Minh who went abroad to study the situation in the world.

"For Ho, Socialists and Communists differed in their policies toward colonies," said the professor, recalling that the young Asian anti-colonialist chose the French Communist Party because the program of Lenin stressed the ending of colonialism whereas the French Social Democrats did not. Next Ho began to build an Association of Vietnamese Revolutionary Young People, believing, as Professor Thong said, that "the advance forces must be young." Ho also stressed the need for an "ideal for the time after independence." He made contact with the Vietnamese nationalist party but judged that it "did not understand the masses."

"In 1930, the Vietnamese Communist Party was founded and soviets were created in two provinces. The emphasis of the Party's line was on the peasant question since ninety percent of the people were peasants. That is why the Party was able to unite the people around it in the Vietminh during World War II. The invading Japanese forces increased the suffering of the people. The 1945 revolution was successful because of its ability to combine armed and political struggle."

Professor Thong concluded: "Ho tried to keep independence for Vietnam within the French Union. Then on September 23, 1945, Resistance began in South Vietnam. This was the beginning of the just war. But we desired peace and that is why Ho Chi Minh went to France for several months. In March, 1946, there was a new treaty. In September, 1946, a Vietnamese representation in France was created which Ho hoped could explain our cause to the French people. We wanted to prevent the French war of aggression. But finally the French began invading. In December, 1946, North Vietnamese Resistance began."

The professor's long discourse took an entire morning. We were impressed by Thong's thoroughness and candor. Heretofore on the trip, we had not been able to raise questions about the controversies and problems emphasized in the West. We asked the professor to speak with us informally about Buddhism and Marxism, and about North Vietnamese-style democracy.

After a hasty lunch, he began to discuss Buddhism and Marxism.

"Buddhism is very old. It was accepted in the eighth century before we won our independence, [and] became a state religion. When the country won its independence, bonzes got good positions in the society. But in the fifteenth century the royal family and king took to the Confucian theory because under Confucianism the king is the head of the country. But the people still continued with Buddhism. The masses have some superstitions, which still remain. People pay very important attention to their ancestors. If you ask what will you do if you die, they make up many different stories.

"The essence of Buddhism is happiness and a peaceful life. It appeals to people to forget themselves. There is a bad aspect of Buddhism. It does not persuade people to participate in social activities. But under certain circumstances it becomes positive. During the civil war, it appealed to people to reject ambitions, called upon us to unite in order to have a happy life as friends and brothers. In a reactionary society a quiet life might follow from Buddhism. But if there are riots or rebels Buddhists may think how to lessen the sufferings of the people. Some may form a revolution, some may sacrifice to make a bright example for others to follow.

"The final ideology of both Buddhism and Marxism, as expressed to me in discussions recently with Japanese Buddhists, is to see the people living in a sane society with happiness and charity, respecting each other. Charity is the love for one another; equality is the respect for one another. Buddhism came into being twenty-five centuries ago; but could not find a way to realize the society it desired. Besides in its history, many regimes made bad use of Buddhism to consolidate their power with superstition. For example, administrations appeal to people to be peaceful and safe, not to follow the revolution even though the people are exploited. Many Buddhists did join the revolution. Many of us lived in pagodas to escape the French. In South Vietnam today, the Buddhists sacrifice themselves to testify to the charity of Buddha. Some Buddhists are very good fighters too," he finished with a smile.

The professor began his earnest description of Vietnamese democracy by noting that it, like Buddhism, precedes Communism in his country's history. He was thinking of government at the village level. "The people in the villages were controlled by a central despotism. But actually the people live and have related to each other within the villages; the relationships within villages and between the village and the central authorities are different things. We have a saying: 'The law of the king is less powerful than the regulation of the village.' The form of living in the village is democratic because everyone is equal. Under feudalism and colonialism, exploitation of the village was easy, but the form of living within it remained democratic."

"In this framework," Thong continued, "people only knew the village. Villagers didn't know anything about despotism. They settled their own affairs within the village provided that they paid some taxes to the state. That is why it was easy for us when we set up people's committees in the villages." Even the French had to recognize the traditional democracy of the village, said the professor, although they attempted to make use of it for their own purposes.

Professor Thong emphasized that part of the village tradition is group decision-making. He insisted that the resolution of differences through constant dialogue is still practiced today. "The West often says we are a dictatorship. But it doesn't understand that we take a very long time in making decisions. For example, the question of increases in salaries. Any worker has the right to question if a fellow worker should get more money. Any worker may appeal to the attorney general if there is something in the work place he doesn't like.

"Many people in fact complain about the time we take to make decisions. We have to guarantee democracy, though, and that is why we take the time. When a question must be decided we come to 'preliminary' or 'temporary' conclusions, but keep respect for contrary ideas. We then organize meetings to reopen discussion. In general, hot discussions occur, but remember we speak very mildly. We speak in an ironic way. We do not put our shoe on the table. As to this there is some difference between North and South Vietnam, but in general even the South Vietnamese are this way. We have a tradition to discuss and negotiate until the end. This works because there is so much unity among the people."[8]

The professor observed that North Vietnam sought to move directly from its traditional village communalism to socialism without an intervening period of capitalism and "bourgeois democracy." He said: "We have not undergone bourgeois democracy. We stand for bypassing this period. The old traditions of democracy may help us advance to socialism. In land reforms and cooperative programs we base ourselves on the tradition of democracy."

This statement led us to inquire about the existence of such "bourgeois democratic" practices as contested elections, jury trial, and freedom of the press. Professor Thong began his response by describing the Socialist and Democratic parties, whose spokesmen we had met at the Fatherland Front offices.

"The people in the cities are very new. They go through a period of bourgeois democracy. That is why the parties [Democratic and Socialist] carry out activities in the cities, to relate the peasant and urban strata. A majority of the peasants

---

[8] Bernard Fall conceded that a draft of the North Vietnamese Constitution of 1960 was sent to popular organizations for wide discussion and amendment before it was adopted. He wrote:

. . . surprisingly enough, it was exactly what its name said: a *project* or a draft, subject to important changes. It is not known whether the imperfections of the document were deliberately "built in" so that later on it would be possible to make it appear that the changes that had been made were the result of public suggestions, or whether the draft was *really* meant to be discussed. The fact remains that the constitution that was finally promulgated on January 1, 1960, showed some marked differences in wording and even in structure from the 1959 draft. (*The Two Viet-Nams*, p. 141).

can follow the Workers Party very easily. People in the cities go through bourgeois democracy. The existence of the Socialist and Democratic parties accustoms these people to the new society. The war against aggression facilitates the ideological growth of these strata. The United Front helps make the town and peasant people feel closer to each other.

"There have been differences between the Marxist-Leninist and the Democratic and Socialist parties. For example, before 1950, in South Vietnam the Democrats had a difference regarding the position of the bourgeoisie in the administration, reflecting the fact that the development of cities in South Vietnam was greater than in North Vietnam. During the Resistance War, cities were encircled. Many who followed the Resistance still had some economic interest in trade between the cities and countryside. The Marxist-Leninist Party had to protect the interest of the peasants, but at the same time pay attention to unity with the landlords who often were lawyers or doctors in the cities. There was discussion and the question was settled. It was not a big problem.

"After peace was made with the French, certain debates also arose about how to advance toward socialism. Members of the Democratic Party wanted the transition prolonged. For instance, they completely approved of the idea of rural cooperatives but did not deeply understand the democratic tradition of the countryside and so wanted a long transition to peasant control. Basically, it was a question of economic interest, specifically of trade between city and country. They also wanted private industry to some extent. It was not a serious conflict though. There was no disagreement among us on foreign policy."

Thong added that there is an important disagreement about what future foreign policy South Vietnam should have. "Some in South Vietnam think neutrality should be very long or forever. In that case, Vietnam would be a confederation not a unified country. If the country unifies, then the South will follow the North or the North will follow the South. Spiritually, North Vietnam belongs to the socialist camp but, in accordance with the Geneva Agreements, it does not belong to any military bloc. At present, due to United States aggression, it is forced to receive arms from wherever possible."

The nature of South Vietnam's foreign policy, the professor stated, "is for the people to decide."

Oanh had said to Tom earlier: "We are socialists, some of them [meaning, we assumed, some of the Buddhists and urban nationalists in South Vietnam] prefer neutrality."

What these Northerners seemed to have in mind was that American withdrawal from South Vietnam would add to the existing forces in the country as a whole a South Vietnamese nationalist bourgeoisie which would possess prestige because it had resisted the Americans. Later, talking to South Vietnamese neutralist Thich Nhat Hahn in New York City, we concluded that an increasing number of South Vietnamese view the situation as do Thong and Oanh, and believe that non-Communist neutralists could survive in peaceful competition with the Communist-led Front if the United States withdrew.

For now and the foreseeable future, however, the Workers Party will lead the revolution. Thong made it clear that the Socialist and Democratic parties have neither the strength nor the desire to achieve majority control of the North Vietnamese government. Their function, rather, is as vehicles for organizing, informing, and consulting urban residents such as property owners and intellectuals concerning policy matters. As Professor Thong's history indicated, the prestige of the Communists grows from the stem of nationalism; there is more than mere propaganda behind the Party slogans, Before you can be a good comrade, you must be a good patriot, and My country is my party. Oanh too had emphasized that the Party's power flows from its leading role in the Resistance, "proof that it has been correct." Communists constitute a minority of the Presidium of the Fatherland Front and the Standing Committee of the National Assembly, we were told, but Oanh said the Party's recommendations rarely are reversed.

We asked about competition between candidates for the National Assembly. Thong answered: "A person must be eighteen [years old] to vote or to be elected. Candidates may stand anywhere they are known, even if it is not their place of residence. Before elections there are consultations among political parties, religious sects, and mass organizations as to candidates. The Front suggests a list which the people may supplement. Some localities have more candidates than offices, others do not. Local committees of the Front may add candidates to those suggested by the central committee. The Socialist and Democratic parties may introduce candidates but not under party names." There is a tendency, said the professor, not to criticize people publicly and to avoid personality fights.[9]

---

[9] Western sources suggest these facts about elections in North Vietnam. The National Assembly was organized in 1946 after elections conducted openly in North and Central Vietnam, the regions under Vietminh authority, and clandestinely in many parts of the French zone in the South. One observer, Robert Scigliano, said that voting "was hardly secret, nor was there much choice among candidates"; another, Lancaster, referred to "some evidence of a readiness to fabricate returns"; further, seventy of the three hundred and fifty seats in the new National Assembly were reserved to nationalist parties by a pre-election deal. On the other hand, "these were the first elections ever held in Vietnam in which the population as a whole was permitted to participate, and the response was enthusiastic." (Robert Scigliano, *South Vietnam: Nation Under Stress* [Boston, 1963], pp. 12–13). And "the results, which gave the Viet Minh a clear majority in the Assembly, were probably fairly indicative of the state of public opinion at that time." (Lancaster, *Emancipation of French Indochina*, p. 127).

During the Resistance the Assembly met only once, to approve a program for land reform, and there were no elections. Not until it was clear beyond question that the national election scheduled for 1956 by the

From Herbert's questioning we learned that some kind of "recall" system operates. The Constitution provides for it, Professor Thong said, and "the Front may suggest to a deputy that he withdraw." After each session of the National As-

---

Geneva Agreements would not take place did North Vietnam draft a new Constitution and, in 1960, hold new Assembly elections. Bernard Fall reported that 458 candidates ran for 404 seats in the National Assembly in 1960, and 448 candidates ran for 366 seats in 1964. (*The Two Viet-Nams*, p. 147; *Viet-Nam Witness* [New York, 1966], p. 127).

One of these authors, Lancaster, also described elections in South Vietnam in 1955. Their purpose was to confirm the dethronement of Bao Dai and the appointment of Ngo Dinh Diem as the Republic's first President. Lancaster said:

The campaign preceding this referendum was conducted with . . . a cynical disregard for decency and democratic principles . . . [In addition to abuse of Bao Dai by the Government-controlled press] police agents and canvassers went from door to door explaining the unpleasant consequences which failure to vote would be likely to entail.

On the day of the referendum polling centres were placed under police surveillance and electors were presented with a ballot paper giving them the choice of voting either for Diem, who was pictured among a group of modern young people against a propitious red background . . . or else for Bao Dai, who was portrayed in old-fashioned robes against an unlucky green background; as an additional precaution, the count was made by government officials without any form of supervision. Under such conditions Diem's victory at the polls was assured, but the final results surpassed even the most sanguine expectations, as the votes cast in some cases exceeded the number of names on the electoral roll. (*The Emancipation of French Indochina*, pp. 398–399).

Another non-Communist Western observer, Denis Warner, described the only other election under Diem, held in 1959 to choose candidates for a South Vietnamese National Assembly. (*The Last Confucian*, pp. 111–112). He said that in the provinces anyone who attempted to run as an opposition candidate was threatened with arrest. In Saigon the Government permitted opposition candidates because of the presence of Westerners, "while taking all precautions to ensure they did not win." One—Dr. Phan Quang Dan—did win, but Diem did not permit him to take his seat.

sembly deputies report back to the people. The Assembly meets twice a year for one or two weeks. When it is not in session, deputies continue their regular occupations, and appear to be most active in their constituencies where they are usually, we were told, members of the people's councils which handle provincial affairs.

Because of the brevity of its meetings, the business of running the National Assembly's affairs seems to fall to its elected Standing Committee. The Assembly also elects a Prime Minister by secret ballot every four years. He in turn presents a Cabinet of ministers for the Assembly's approval. When "big problems" arise between meetings of the Assembly, said the professor, they are laid before a Council of Government including all ministers and vice-ministers, which exchanges views with the Standing Committee.

In response to questions about the judicial system, the professor said: "The Civilian Control Institute, and the president of the Supreme Court, are elected by the National Assembly independently of the Government. The state then approves judges recommended by the Supreme Court. In the courts are representatives of local people. They have the power to discuss with the court the extent of punishment to be given or whether or not the individual is guilty."

Trial procedure requires both prosecuting and defense attorneys, he said. We asked if they agree with the assumption that a person is innocent until proven guilty.

"We generally assume so," he replied. He had a difficult time understanding our point, and finally added: "We are young and have not enough regulations. We base ourselves mostly on our traditions and our Constitution. But there is not so much trouble because everything is discussed."

Asked if confession is sufficient evidence for conviction, he said: "This has not been established. In general we get this from the French tradition."[10]

Tom tried to ask if informal pressures, such as the prestige of leaders, force people to conform with majority opinion in their thinking. The professor said that he thought that the existence of different opinions would in itself ensure that discussions continue.

But he said of Ho Chi Minh: "He knows he has prestige. That is why he is careful when he speaks. If something is unclear to him, he tries not to give an opinion. As far as articles are concerned, many people want to write in beautiful and complex words. Ho criticizes them but they go on. What the President says is just advice. To follow or not, is up to you."

---

[10] In 1952 Starobin met a lawyer at the Vietminh jungle headquarters who had been a legal adviser to Ho's delegation to France in 1946. Vu Trong Khanh told him the following:

"I was very proud of my profession as a lawyer. But it has taken me the six years of the Resistance to understand the true meaning of the law. Consider the problem of crime in our countryside. What was the punishment? Payments of fine, perhaps prison. And then the criminal might very well resume his past. Now I have understood that such problems as misery and lack of education cannot be cured by fines and prisons. It requires raising the standard of living and increasing production, as our government is teaching us to do.

"Now, in liberated areas, when a crime is committed—let us say, a robbery—the culprit is brought before all the villagers. It is they who decide to re-educate him. They take the matter in their own hands. Assuming that his crime is serious enough to merit prison, he must do useful work there. He must meditate. His cultural level must be raised. In leaving prison, he has understood why the robbery was committed. He does not usually become a lawbreaker again. This difference in penology—why, it's a difference in systems!" (*Eyewitness in Indo-China*, p. 136).

For better or worse, these remarks appear to suggest the spirit underlying Professor Thong's comments about justice.

Tom asked if the professor himself ever disagreed with Ho. Thong, laughing, shot back: "So far, I have not."

At various times we also discussed the North Vietnamese "system" with our interpreters, Oanh and Hieu. Oanh had this to say of the police: "Most of them are looking after the security and order of the transportation and communications. As for the security and order of the population, the people themselves look after it. An example—in Hanoi we are divided into many quarters, like 'districts' in Europe, where the people elect a body of five or six in charge of order and security. They organize the secure life of the population and look after every aspect of the daily life without the necessity of causing difficulties for the administration; sort of a people's administration in the quarter. Children, for instance, after school, they used to run in the streets and everywhere, and are very undisciplined. Playing football on the streets, and so forth. It is an obstacle for communications. People of this body go around the street, advise the children to go back home at noon to sleep, save their health and not cause trouble."

Tom inquired about what occurs when disagreements are not easily overcome. Oanh at first thought we were referring to antisocial "obstinate elements," whom he said are fewer and fewer in number. "The longer they receive the counsels of the masses, the better they know what is democracy and how to solve questions. We don't see difficult problems which cannot be solved through discussions and consultations." Explaining his conception of democracy in the case of a "small thing," he said, "Suppose someone finds something foreign on the street —a fountain pen or anything interesting—and he gathers his friends about how to solve. The best way is to give it to the people's council of the quarter. They would decide this will be put up somewhere, and they will call on people who lost pens to come and take it, if it is theirs."

Later while we drank Vietnamese beer at the restaurant overhanging the lake, we began describing conflicts between the generations in America to learn if similar conflicts occurred in Vietnam. Staughton described American "beatniks" and reported our impression that similar social groups are emerging in Eastern Europe. As with all comparisons to Western societies, Oanh minimized the parallels. He said many young Vietnamese enjoy "modern music" of the kind being played over the restaurant radio. "The younger generation likes this sound more than the classical sound," he said, but added that the problem is different from that in Eastern Europe. "It is not a question of resisting the authority of the older generation. Only question is whether to restore the national tradition of culture or not. The young people only pay attention to things that are immediate and they forget the traditions, but it is the line of the Party to restore all that is purely traditional Vietnamese. The Party encourages new plays which conform to the demands of the struggle at the present time, but at the same time these plays should be based on the tradition of the classic opera, which is popular in the whole country. The young people wish to create new forms of theater, opera, but they only think of the new forms while they forget the characteristic of the national culture, and they don't make a profound study of what is purely Vietnamese. Without a profound study of the classical poem, however, you cannot create new forms—do you see what I mean?"

Whether this "conflict" was one between generations, or whether it represented an indirect criticism by youth of certain tendencies of the Party, we never determined. We returned instead to the questions that have created political conflicts in other socialist societies. How fast should industrialization proceed? When should agriculture be collectivized? In foreign policy, how important is it to aid other revolutions at the expense of building up one's own country? Again, Oanh indicated that such issues were not crucial in Vietnam because of the particular "characteristic" of his society. "Since the Vietnamese people have been struggling many centuries under foreign domination, they eagerly desire independence, progress, revolution, everything that is progress is welcomed by the large majority of people. That is why the contradiction is not as heavy as arises in other countries between different classes within the revolution. Also the degree of oppression here has been much heavier than on other peoples. This is why the majority wants progress. The problems of industrialization, collectivization—everything—are warmly welcomed. This is why when a policy is put forward by the Government and Party, the discussion around such problems is not as acute as in the case of other countries. For example, in the Soviet Union, the struggle between the proletariat and the capitalist class is quite another thing. In Russia before the Revolution the capitalist class was completely opposing the working class, while in Vietnam the socialist transformation of the capitalist class is quite different. We consider the capitalist class as allies, coming within the ranks of the people and combined with the rest of the people in resisting foreign aggression. From that, we can understand other problems which can be solved in a peaceful way in the class struggle in Vietnam. In the long run, it is only a problem of explaining to those people who will understand fully the problem. When they are convinced, and when they know the Party has served their interest by bringing them independence, they will be very quick to understand their interest in all things, and so the main problem is to increase the explanation of policy to these people."

Staughton later asked Hieu to clarify how the "Party line" develops and is applied in local situations. Hieu said the "lower level" discusses the general line, whether or not to agree with it, then they discuss how to put it into practice. "Not all the people are Party members," Hieu said, adding that individuals must apply for membership and be accepted by the "collectivity," or cell, which ranges in size from three to as many as seventy persons. But the non-Party people in every locality "can have a voice." "Whatever they want to, they discuss together and come to conclusions together. If something must be done in an urgent way," he said, echoing Professor Thong, "they may take some preliminary decision to smooth the work. Then the people who disagree may raise and discuss the problem again, or ask for the decision to be improved. Very simple."

6

MEETING
AN AMERICAN
PRISONER

The Vietnamese consider captured U.S. pilots war criminals whose Government has not declared war and whose actions constitute "war crimes" and "crimes against humanity" as defined by the Nuremberg Tribunal after World War II. But—and each time this phrase was used the intense, slight men who said it seemed to draw themselves up with quiet dignity—"we are a humane people." Although American prisoners are believed to have no rights as prisoners of war because war has not been declared, they choose to treat them adequately.

This generalization apparently holds for the Front as well. In May, 1965, an important defector from the N.L.F. forces— a member of the Lao Dong (Communist) Party of North Vietnam and a junior officer, who had joined the Vietminh in 1949 at the age of fifteen—testified after his defection that his unit had orders not to beat any prisoner of war. Seymour Topping reported:

"If they were wounded seriously we took care of them on the spot and gave them a propaganda talk before leaving them," Dau said. American prisoners got better treatment than Vietnamese and had to be turned over to higher headquarters immediately.[1]

Oanh and others in North Vietnam told us that during the Resistance against the French, French prisoners received more food than soldiers in the Vietminh Army.

We made several inquiries about seeing U.S. prisoners of war, if only to bring back tapes to their relatives. The Army finally granted permission to see one man.

The evening began with a one-hour discussion between ourselves and two D.R.V. soldiers at our hotel. We were awkward, not quite knowing how to proceed with questions or what to expect. They were solicitous that our wishes and customs be respected during the interview. They said they hoped we somehow could explain the war to the prisoner.

We were tense and doubtful about the propriety of the meeting. In general, we identify with anyone behind bars rather than with his captors; we oppose capital punishment. And this prisoner was a fellow American. We were uncertain about our ability to communicate even friendship to an Air Force pilot who, we thought, probably believed the American peace movement was inspired by a pack of draft dodgers. Tom feared that decency compelled us to leave the man in peace and not humiliate him further. Staughton thought that there was at least a chance that we could communicate a message from the prisoner to his family.

Arriving at the Fatherland Front office where the interview

[1] *New York Times*, May 23, 1965.

was to be held, the three of us were united by new anxieties. As we entered, movie cameras were grinding, arousing our fears that the interview would be turned into a propaganda show. In the room itself, there were three tables with cups, saucers, candy, and cigarettes, one each for the Army representatives, ourselves, and the prisoner. However, we were shocked and dismayed to find the prisoner's table set at a lower level than ours, and with a stool in place of a chair. We explained to our hosts that this was an arrangement that we could not accept, based as it was on an assumption of the evildoing of the individual American pilot. It seemed to us that such an arrangement would make trust or communication impossible. The reply, a vague one, was that the pilot was a "criminal," and that the Vietnamese wanted to preserve a distinction between the American "friends" and the American "criminal." We tried several times to explain, each time with increasing respect for their tolerance of our pleas for this pilot who had bombed their country. Finally they gave us a proper chair, and removed the cameras, but the lower table remained as a sign of the distinction.

We asked for time to talk among ourselves. Herbert said that, had we known beforehand, we could have declined politely, but that as the informal "leader" it would be improper for him to refuse at this point. He suggested, however, that if Staughton or Tom wished, we could leave. Both of us were deeply disturbed by the situation, and Staughton at one point said he preferred to leave. Tom shared this emotion, but he also thought that it might be unfair to leave Herbert to explain to the Vietnamese and the pilot. Staughton eventually agreed, and we nervously took our seats.

An armed soldier entered to announce that the prisoner was outside. Before we realized it, the American was in the room. A man of medium height and fair complexion, he wore a heavy black sweater and green fatigues. We immediately stood and shook hands with him while the Vietnamese watched. We could barely keep our hands from trembling. The sensation of being an American, allied with an "enemy," talking with the "American criminal," was nearly insufferable. We had seen thousands of men with faces like this one, but he was the first we had encountered as a prisoner in a conflict where we, objectively, were on another side.

The prisoner did not help us to feel any more relaxed. He seemed to be grappling for self-control too. His opening phrases were cautious, even mechanical. "How are you? . . . I believe you, Dr. Lynd, are a historian at Yale; you, Mr. Hayden, work with some student committees; and you, Dr. Aptheker, are a journalist of some kind, though I'm sorry I can't say that I've read any of your books." He gave us a blinking, testing gaze.

Herbert told him that we were Americans who opposed the war, that we had been able to arrange this meeting through the D.R.V. Army, and that we were permitted to take back a message to the prisoner's family. Tom described his work in Newark, explained how he had become interested in the war, and expressed his sympathy for the prisoner's situation. Staughton described his work at Yale, said he thought the U.S. was on the wrong side of a social revolution in Vietnam, and pledged his word of honor that we would not use politically any message the pilot wanted to send home.

After about five minutes we had warmed to each other. And we felt growing respect for this American who took greater and greater command of his emotions as the minutes passed.

He told us he had been a pilot for several years, and before that a student in the South. He had a large family, including several small children, and felt terribly lonely for them, especially since this is the "age when they are really forming their opinions." It was evident that he was a man who worked in the Air Force as a means of a good living, not primarily for ideological reasons. He did a job, hoping and trusting that his Government's policies were correct and just. He knew little about Vietnam, but said he remembered a "teach-in" and "regretted" not having listened to it. Now he learned about Vietnam from the only reading permitted him, the *Vietnam Courier*, an English-language newspaper edited from the viewpoint of the D.R.V. Government, and from the English-language Radio Hanoi.

It was his fifth month in jail since being shot down—"on my first mission." It was hard to realize that we would be boarding a plane soon, landing three days later in the United States, and that this man would still pace a small cell hoping, as he told us, that "this ends as soon as possible."

He was, the pilot said, adequately clothed and fed, and he mentioned in particular a turkey dinner at Christmas. He told us that he showers every day. He has been allowed to write one letter to his family, and hopes soon to be able to write one each month. He said the Vietnamese for the most part left him to himself.

But, the prisoner told us simply, his treatment while better than he had expected was "no bed of roses." The one point in our discussion at which he seemed upset was when we told him that the two U.S. Army non-commissioned officers released by the N.L.F. at Thanksgiving were being held incommunicado in Okinawa. The pilot said nothing, but earlier remarks made it clear that he had hoped other prisoner releases might follow.

As the allowed hour drew to a close, the prisoner half-humorously chatted with his Army captors about taking fruit and candy back to his cell. The permission granted, he ungraciously but bravely put the candy and fruit up his sleeves, stood and thanked us a bit too abruptly, turned his back, and was gone.

The prisoner requested that we communicate to his wife and children through her brother. Staughton carried out his commission when we returned to the United States. They had not known if the pilot was alive or dead.

The Australian Communist reporter, Wilfred Burchett, spoke with three captured pilots in spring, 1966. All reported "adequate" food and medical care, and one, Major Lawrence Guarino, USN, mentioned a turkey dinner at Christmas as had the man with whom we spoke.[2] Despite pictures of captured American pilots being paraded through the streets of Hanoi which appeared in the newspapers in the early summer and despite rumors of impending executions, in October, 1966, a high State Department official stated that "there's no indication of brutality or mistreatment" and a Defense Department source echoed: "No brainwashing—apparently no torture."[3]

[2] Wilfred G. Burchett, *Vietnam North* (New York, 1966), Chapter 2.
[3] *New York Times,* October 12, 1966.

7

PEACE NEGOTIATIONS I:
WHAT THE OTHER SIDE WANTS

I

Before leaving the United States, Staughton wrote a brief memorandum entitled "Things Which Need Clarification About the N.L.F.–Hanoi Negotiating Position." The memorandum posited that two points were particularly unclear. One was the other side's conception of the political future of South Vietnam. At issue were (and are) whether or not the N.L.F. would be willing to have other representatives of the South Vietnamese people at a peace conference, and whether a coalition government would be formed before or after elections for a new National Assembly. The second problem, murky in the United States, was whether or not the other side insisted on the withdrawal of all American troops before peace talks.

En route to Hanoi we raised these and similar questions at every encounter with Front and North Vietnamese personnel.

Much of Staughton's time on the Hanoi-bound planes was spent, Czech portable typewriter on knees, attempting to distill the results of these conversations and to formulate the best questions to ask in North Vietnam.

As our small propeller-driven plane flew the last lap into Hanoi from Nanning, Staughton tentatively phrased answers to the two points which had seemed unclear before leaving the United States. In each case what had emerged from talks in Prague, Moscow, and Peking was not a formula but a new perspective. Regarding the political future of South Vietnam, the other side's attitude was clearly that concessions had been made in the past and concessions could be made again, yet that in principle the destiny of South as of North Vietnam was a matter for only Vietnamese to settle. Concerning troop withdrawal, it now seemed that the alternatives had been posed wrongly in America. In the United States one asked: do they want the withdrawal of all troops before negotiations, or would an agreement on the principle of ultimate withdrawal be enough? What emerged from our conversations was that the other side wants neither one nor the other. They are concerned that America *decide* to withdraw, as the French had in the past; that any plans for permanent military bases be abandoned. Once made, this decision could be communicated by whatever "actual deed" of de-escalation America chose.

Thinking of all this, Staughton wrote: "Thus far, my impression is that no gimmick, no diplomatic skill, no offer of discrete concessions, and no amount of military power can bring this dreadful war to an end. The 'other side' wants one thing, and they will fight to the death for it: America must decide to withdraw." Negotiation both about South Vietnam's government and American troop withdrawal was possible, and considerable flexibility might be expected in details, but only in the context of United States recognition that it had no right to be present in Vietnam in the first place.

II

During the first half of our stay in North Vietnam, the most significant further clarification of negotiating positions came on January 1. That morning in the former residence of Madame Nhu, we met with Colonel Ha Van Lau, representative of the People's Army to the International Control Commission, and now a member of the D.R.V. committee to decide on procedure toward captured American pilots. The Colonel said: "The Geneva Agreements were a victory in the struggle to achieve our national rights, a struggle against the French backed by the U.S. The basic goals were sovereignty, independence, unity, and territorial integrity for Vietnam, Laos, and Cambodia. Now I'll tell you of the spirit and letter of Geneva.

"Politically, the Agreements provided a time limit for re-unification, respect for democratic liberties, and that foreign powers should not intervene. The cessation of hostilities was to be carried out in the first stage. Other provisions were to consolidate peace: no troops, no bases, no military alliance; guarantee the buffer character of the seventeenth parallel, a provisional division, not a political or territorial boundary.

"The Agreements conformed to our fundamental national rights against imperialist policies of aggression and war.

"The cessation of hostilities was signed by the French and ourselves. The U.S. did not sign although they helped the French. They were not officially 'belligerent.' The Agreements were not signed by other participants, but they agreed to abide by them. Therefore, the U.S. is bound legally. Moreover,

Bedell Smith said the U.S. 'took note' of the Agreements and pledged not to disturb them.

"During the first three hundred days there was to be regroupment of troops. This was correctly implemented. Since then, each side has implemented the Agreements in a different way. Consultations, we agreed, were to be in July, 1955, and elections in July, 1956. But Eisenhower planned to turn South Vietnam into a separate state, a new-type colony. We have authentic documents on American intervention in Vietnam.

"On August 4, 1953, Eisenhower stated at a Governor's Conference: 'If we lose Indochina, it will be difficult to save the rest of the Southeast Asian peninsula. We would lose tin which we highly value. We have spent four hundred million for this war to meet our material needs in Southeast Asia.' " He added, "This was before Geneva. This was the economic need.

"On January 13, 1954, Dulles stated that the interest of the U.S. in the Far East from a strategic point of view is closely linked with the chain of offshore islands: Korea in the north and, if possible, Indochina in the south, Japan, Taiwan, New Zealand, and Australia. They wanted to occupy South Vietnam as a basis for conquest of Indochina.

"On July 20, 1954, Eisenhower said he was not bound by the Agreements just when Smith was giving the accords support. Then the U.S. set up SEATO with South Vietnam, Laos, and Cambodia included in its protected area. Diem wanted to join SEATO formally but did not dare because of the Geneva prohibition against military alliances.

"There were four stages during implementation of the Geneva Agreements: 1954–56, 1956–60, 1961–64, 1965–present.

"In the first stage, after regroupment the two sides should have carried out the political provisions. Our Government put

North Vietnam

forward numerous proposals for elections, but at the instigation of the U.S., Diem refused. He gave an unfounded pretext, saying he did not sign and therefore was not bound. But the French signed. The real cause, clear from even the press, was that if elections were held ninety percent of South Vietnam would vote for Ho Chi Minh.

"On May 8, 1956, the Soviet Union and England, co-chairmen of the Geneva Conference, sent a message requesting an election. The South Vietnam Administration turned down that request. The U.S. Government kicked out the French, then got in deeper and deeper.

"In 1955, Diem used armed forces to suppress religious sects that had been pro-French. A March on the North slogan was raised, and there was a buildup of puppet troops. There was U.S.–Diem ruthless repression right from the beginning. Under the slogan of fighting Communism, Diem struck at old patriots who sought peace and reunification.

"The French expeditionary force withdrew in April, 1956. The U.S. Military Advisory Group came in.

"The ICC carried out effective activities in this period, investigating many violations, especially reprisals against former Resistance members. They found no violations by North Vietnam.

"Second stage: U.S. buildup of airlines, highways; purpose, not just to suppress the people's movement but to prepare a base in Southeast Asia. North Vietnam proposed normal relations, freedom of correspondence and movement, in economic and cultural areas, but they would not accept these proposals. Instead, they constructed a network of concentration camps and hamlets.

"In December, 1958, the Phu Loi concentration camp held six thousand persons.

"In 1959, Diem began saying there was a state of war.

Americans allowed him to carry out massacres. Faced with this, the people waged a political struggle for democratic liberties and implementation of the Geneva Agreements.

"Diem was comparable to the Middle Ages. There were only two alternatives: either to be slaves or rise up and defend the right to live. In 1960, the N.L.F. was born.

"The third period was 1961–64, from military intervention to armed aggression by special war.

"In 1961, a [Vice-President] Johnson-Diem joint communi-qué gave legal cover to U.S. intervention. A new-type war of aggression was consistent with new-type colonialism. The two main features were: one, terrorist operations; and, two, the strategic hamlet program. 'Mopping up' operations were de-signed to crush patriotic armed forces. People were herded into hamlets to get them under control. The main force to be used was the puppet [i.e., South Vietnamese] Army. The U.S. was to be in an advisory role. The U.S. said this is a Vietnamese war, a civil war. It is so because Diem's Army is fighting against the people of South Vietnam.

"The first strategic hamlet plan was to pacify people in eighteen months. But in 1962, the plan was prolonged up until 1963. They could not wipe out political forces in South Vietnam. The plan provided for seventeen thousand hamlets in which ten million would be herded. The policy of hamlets was regarded as the backbone of special war. To win, they must control the population. They must do it by force. In the end they could only build eight thousand such hamlets. These too are being destroyed by the people. The struggle lasted for years and was very hard. The population was compelled by the troops, as in concentration camps.

"It was political and armed struggle combined then. The people had much guerrilla experience against the French. Kill-ing Diem marked the end of this strategy. McNamara did not give up, however. He came to South Vietnam in 1964–65 with the hope of continuing the war. His new plan was based on failure of the Staley-Taylor plan [for strategic hamlets].

"The new plan was to extend the war to the North. It was meant to retrieve the critical situation in South Vietnam where the U.S. faced imminent defeat. The U.S. never mentioned Geneva Agreements up to that time because they knew their actions were contrary to them.

"On June 2, 1962, in order to get legal cover after Johnson's May, 1961, statement, they got the ICC to make a majority report. In that the Indian and Canadian majority said North Vietnam was engaging in subversive and aggressive acts. This was drawn up on the basis of false reports given to them by South Vietnam. There was no investigation of these reports. This whole ICC report was contrary to the principle of unanimous decision and the practice of investigating before coming to conclusions.

"As these plans were deteriorating Johnson became President. A new period began in 1965. He sent [Maxwell D.] Taylor to South Vietnam. There was a change of U.S. strategy: first, U.S. troops to South Vietnam; second, extend the war to North Vietnam; third, peace offensive.

"At the beginning of 1964 there were thirty thousand U.S. troops and advisers. Now there are over one hundred and eighty thousand, not counting the Seventh Fleet and troops in Guam and Thailand.

"South Vietnam is a testing ground for American special war. Now the U.S. is testing the latest-type weapons, poison gases, artillery, and planes. Many kinds are now being tested. U.S. troops commit countless crimes in South Vietnam. You know about their countless crimes—even some U.S. troops protest against them. There is a letter from twenty American soldiers. Some officers and soldiers commit suicide because of the deception. I haven't their names.

"Sent to defend freedom, now they realize they are fighting against those they should defend. They even gas children hiding in shelters. They practice saturation bombing."

Herbert broke in to ask if the Colonel knew of any American defections. Before continuing his exposition, Ha Van Lau responded: "I know of no instance of a U.S. soldier switching sides."

Then he said: "Now the revolutionary Army is winning big battles. Hand-to-hand action prevents the use of air support. The U.S. Army is a modern, regular one, but South Vietnam has many marshes and forests, and a people's war is being fought against them. Therefore, from any viewpoint, it is not suitable. That is why U.S. troops are being beaten in South Vietnam.

"The fundamental point is politics and morale. The U.S. Army is in great difficulty with logistics and support because they are very heavy. At Pleiku, a U.S. battalion was wiped out. At Da Nang and Chu Lai, fourteen thousand could not intervene to save a South Vietnamese regiment from annihilation.

"In the political field, the LBJ–Taylor plan called for civilian administration. But Ky is the weakest, most hated person they've had, with the least international support. There is an insuperable internal contradiction. It is the offspring of the U.S. policy of aggression and war. The rate of desertion increased: eighty-four thousand in 1964; ninety thousand in the first nine months of 1965—about ten thousand per month according to the U.S. press. The U.S. divides the Vietnamese into many groups. It is impossible for them to consolidate a government. U.S. policy is to support one clique, keep another in the wings, and this causes the contradiction. So Taylor was recalled and [Henry Cabot] Lodge sent to replace Ky with a civilian, but he was unable to because it runs against Ky's personal interest.

"They are not patriots. That is why the people of South Vietnam have hated them.

"There is some evidence of mutiny: instances of company revolts against the puppet Army and of a battalion which disobeyed orders to go on. The intervention of U.S. troops has aroused the nationalist spirit. A danger of mutiny? Yes, from the national point of view there are antagonistic contradictions. Chiang's troops had been heavily armed by the U.S., but when the Liberation Army came to south China they fled.

"It is impossible to increase the puppet Army. Saigon controls five million people, about five hundred thousand soldiers. The desertion rate is one of every four or five, the highest in the world.

"The war has been extended to the North in order to bring pressure on the D.R.V. to negotiate on American terms. The air war in the North is different from the South, but is the same in the sense of violating the integrity of our country.

"At first LBJ said he would aim only at steel. But the U.S. Air Force strikes at any object, day and night. They change methods and forms of attacks, hit any moving objective. Even the leprosarium, hundreds of schools, churches, pagodas, towns such as Vinh, industrial plants. This only increases our determination. We have downed eight hundred and fifty planes. Heavier still is the political defeat suffered by the U.S. It is the sacred duty of all Vietnamese to safeguard the Fatherland. The whole people now are unified.

"Is North Vietnam aggressing against South Vietnam? Ridiculous. LBJ comes from thousands of miles away to invade people in the North who are helping and supporting the South—are they aggressing against themselves? The right to defend the Fatherland conforms to the Geneva Agreements.

"The peace offensive is parallel to President Johnson's Johns Hopkins speech. Its strategic significance is that it is part of a new aggressive plan. In view of military defeats, the U.S. is compelled to send in troops, making the U.S. appear to be the aggressor in the eyes of the world. Now they seek negotiations from a position of strength. The so-called unconditional discussions, or returning to the Geneva accords, are their main points. But always on U.S. terms. The U.S. says it will keep its pledge to South Vietnam, and it plans to replace the French in the role they played at Geneva.

"The Four Points of the D.R.V. are based on Geneva and on the actual situation in South Vietnam over the last eleven years. The U.S. sabotaged peace. The Five Points of the N.L.F. are based on the same theory.

"We expect support from the American people, finally. The situation in Vietnam is extremely dangerous. The root cause is U.S. imperialist aggression and war. We request that the U.S. accepts the Four Points and proves it by concrete actions, practical actions. There will be many sacrifices and hardships. But we are confident of unity here, support in the world, contradictions in the U.S. and imperialist camp. We have small propaganda means compared to LBJ, but we have many friends in many countries."

After this long survey, the Colonel asked us to lunch. The company included the chairman of the Peace Committee as well as Oanh, its permanent secretary. Over the bamboo shoots and hot sauces, we asked question after question. Ha Van Lau answered with these comments:

"On coalition and elections, one must take their [the Americans'] statements as a whole. They use the term 'self-determination' to cover their purposes.

"At Geneva our delegation proposed six months after regroupment as the interim period before elections. The compromise was to have a consultative conference after one year and elections after two. The seventeenth parallel was also a compromise, to be removed after two years. All parties pledged to respect this. They also agreed on article fourteen C, out of fear of reprisals by Diem.

"I was at Geneva. I remember well on July twentieth, it was after five P.M. and we had been asking for the fifteenth parallel and the French asked the eighteenth. Krishna Menon of India proposed the seventeenth. Hue and Da Nang are between the fifteenth and seventeenth, four provinces altogether, three and a half million people who were Resistance fighters. We could have continued fighting. The French were disintegrating. But this way we stopped the process of U.S. intervention by atomic bombing. The main point was to check the U.S. maneuver of prolonging and expanding the war."

When Staughton asked that the Colonel specify ways by which the war might be ended, the Colonel responded with two important points: 1. "withdraw newly arrived units"; 2. "recognize the N.L.F."

Nonnegotiable, he said, are the principles of peace, independence, democracy, and national unity. "Concrete details" can be negotiated, but must be discussed on the basis of accepting that peace means independence, he added.

Staughton advised that in the U.S. people think that there can be no free election in a Communist society, and asked, "How did the D.R.V. imagine the elections of 1956?"

The Colonel said: "Geneva stipulated: one, universal suffrage; two, secret ballot; three, international supervision. We felt these would be sufficient."

We asked if there would have been an opposition candidate to Ho. The Vietnamese all laughed.

"It would have been hard because Ho is our national leader," said the Colonel, comparing Ho to George Washington.

One professor from the Peace Committee said: "Now in

South Vietnam, the N.L.F. is liberating and the U.S. is bombing, so if there is an election, who will the people vote for?"

III

This root fact of the Front's confidence in its support by the South Vietnamese people affects its position on two matters widely discussed in the United States: amnesty and elections.

What is the position of the N.L.F. on amnesty?

The program of the Front in 1960 stated that there should be "all democratic freedoms": of expression, of the press, of assembly, of association, of movement, of religious belief, and "freedom of action to all patriotic political parties and mass organizations, irrespective of political tendency." It called for a general amnesty to all political detainees and the abolition of concentration camps. Most pertinently, it said: "Strictly ban all illegal arrests and imprisonments, tortures and corporal punishment. Punish unrepentant murderers of the people."

In the *Vietnam Courier* for November 4, 1965, the "main contents" of the Front's policy toward puppet troops, as "repeatedly stated," are said to be:

1. "Punish with a steady hand" a "very few officers and thugs who deliberately follow the U.S. aggressors and massacre and murder the people."

2. Welcome deserters who return to their families. They will be entitled to land, and rewarded if they bring their arms with them.

3. Units who break away from the puppet Army and wish to join the Army of the Front as units may do so.

4. As to the puppet officers, the Front anticipates their playing an active role if they stand up boldly to struggle for

peace and neutrality. The Front is prepared to work with all individuals and units "who, for political reasons, under the threat of a purge by the U.S. imperialists and their lackeys, are willing to get out of their control."

Beyond this, we received a strong impression of the D.R.V.'s skill in finding a place within its various organizations for previously antagonistic groups. International supervision of amnesty remains important but less so than if the Front were in fact seeking to force its will on a basically hostile populace.

The problem of elections also appears in a new light when we recall that a group need not fear elections if it expects to win them. Involved here, of course, is the third point of the four-point basis for negotiations set forward by Prime Minister Pham Van Dong on April 8, 1965, in response to President Johnson's Johns Hopkins speech. The third point calls for settling the affairs of South Vietnam in accord with the program of the National Liberation Front. As James Leonard, Deputy Director of Far Eastern Research for the State Department, told Staughton after our return, even the United States Government "sits around wondering what this means."

What is the meaning of settling the affairs of South Vietnam according to the program of the National Liberation Front?

The 1960 program of the Front calls for the formation of a "national democratic coalition government."

Since then, this passage has been amplified. The first Congress of the N.L.F. in 1962 declared: "All mass organizations and political parties regardless of political tendency or religious creed are guaranteed freedom of organization and action as well as freedom of presenting candidates to the National Assembly and to other elected bodies. The Front undertakes to . . . dissolve the present National Assembly and hold another parliamentary election in an honest and genuinely democratic way." Since the 1960 program speaks of electing "a new National Assembly through universal suffrage," it can be assumed that universal suffrage is intended by the 1962 declaration.

At the second Congress of the N.L.F., President Nguyen Huu Tho delivered a speech on January 1, 1964, which quoted the N.L.F. Central Committee as having raised as one of six urgent demands on November 8, 1963, after the fall of Diem, "that the parties concerned in South Vietnam negotiate with one another to reach cease-fire and solve the important problems of the nation."

However, it must be clear that the present Saigon regime is not regarded by the N.L.F. as one of the "parties concerned." In his interview with *Asahi*, Nguyen Huu Tho stated: "It represents nobody and is scorned by the South Vietnamese people and the world people."

Are these Front declarations simply window dressing?

Not according to South Vietnamese neutralists interviewed by recent American visitors. For example, I. F. Stone spoke with a lawyer who also is a high official in the South Vietnamese civil service. "There is no way out," he said, "except to recognize and negotiate with the National Liberation Front." Yet he was hopeful that the Front would not insist on Communism or reunification. The official told Stone: "If the U.S. recognizes the Front, invites it to a conference, and proposes a republican government, I believe the Front will accept this so long as the regime is non-aligned, and represents all political tendencies including the Communists."

Similar sentiments were expressed to Stone by another South Vietnamese non-Communist, the Buddhist monk Thich Nhat Hanh. "The VC [Vietcong] prefer political to military means," Hanh stated. "I believe they would accept a cease-fire. They feel that the current peace moves are not genuine. The thing to do is to stop the bombings North and South, stop all offensive military action, and do it sincerely and the other side will reciprocate."[1] Later, in New York City, we heard these same sentiments from Hanh in person.

Stone's impressions are corroborated by the six-man pacifist group who went to Saigon in mid-April, 1966, under the leadership of A. J. Muste. One of the group, Catholic Karl Meyer, talked with a Catholic priest who said that most of his nine thousand parishioners want peace rather than a continuation of the war, even though 80 percent of them are refugees from North Vietnam. Bradford Lyttle, a veteran of pacifist demonstrations, reported the feelings of something like one hundred South Vietnamese non-Communists as follows:

. . . while many of these people feared communism or outside influence they would rather take their chances with them than continue the war, a puppet government and endless killing.

Most felt that a coalition government could be set up in South Vietnam that with U.S. economic and technical aid could remain democratic and independent.

All expressed respect for the NLF and "Viet Cong": "For after all, they are fighting for the country's independence. They are patriots."[2]

The most extensive account of the findings of the mission of the Committee for Nonviolent Action came from Muste himself.[3] Muste said: "In the opinion of many responsible Vietnamese, if U.S. support were withdrawn, the Ky regime would be replaced by a civilian regime composed of Buddhists, Roman Catholics, intellectuals, peasant representatives. . . . Such a civilian set-up—again according to our contacts—would favor

[1] *I. F. Stone's Weekly*, May 16, 1966.
[2] *The Peacemaker*, May 14, 1966; *CNVA Bulletin*, May 2, 1966.
[3] "A Visit to Saigon," *Liberation*, Summer, 1966.

a cease-fire in the civil war and be ready to sit down to talk with the N.L.F. and the Vietcong."

Muste paraphrased the responses of South Vietnamese non-Communists to typical American objections to a coalition government with Communists:

The first goes like this: "Suppose this proved true—the take-over, even the purge—then how do you figure that it is for the White House and the Pentagon to decide whether we Viet-namese are to run the risk? Furthermore, if allegedly to avoid this catastrophe, you continue to bomb and kill non-Communist Vietnamese in order to 'protect' them from Communists, why do you think this is going to make us love *you?* In fact, every bomb you drop will make more enemies for you."

A second comment ran like this: "We do not anticipate such a take-over and purge because the masses want to live in peace after all these years. No element which provokes violence, once a cease-fire is achieved, will get anywhere with them. Besides, the war has taken its toll of the Vietcong too and they also want a respite."

Still another argument pointed out that if a coalition regime came into being the non-Communist elements in it would carry great weight, because they would have had a decisive share in bringing peace and getting U.S. troops out of the country, something that the Vietcong by solely military force cannot accomplish.

Lastly, our informants said: "You Americans must not think that we regard the Vietcong as foreigners and you as Viet-namese! The Vietcong are our countrymen. They are patriots according to their own lights. They have fought against foreigners." And invariably they came back with the chal-lenge: "Who are the Americans that they should decide our destiny for us? We want them as friends and helpers, not as killers, on our soil."

Those who regard N.L.F. references to elections in South Vietnam as window dressing point to the fact that throughout 1965, as in the speech of Prime Minister Pham Van Dong on

April 8, the other side characterized the Front as the "sole authentic representative" of the South Vietnamese people which would require a "decisive voice" in any peace settlement. Does this not mean, some analysts demand, that the Front insists on *de facto* supremacy for itself before any elections are held?

This is not necessarily true. For while the Front has styled itself the only proper spokesman for the South Vietnamese people, the United States has refused to deal directly with the Front at all. The fourteen points put forward by President Johnson during the peace offensive move toward the position of the other side on every issue but this one. No longer does the United States repudiate the Geneva Agreements, no longer does it insist that South Vietnam is an independent sovereign state. Yet, in point thirteen, the fiction still is maintained that the Front is a mere creature of the North Vietnamese Government and could have its views represented at a peace conference only as part of the North Vietnamese delegation. Therefore, what we have no way of knowing is whether or not, if America agreed to deal directly with the Front, the other side would drop its insistence on the Front as the only political spokesman for the South and tacitly agree to interpret the D.R.V. point three in the minimal sense of direct contact rather than in the maximal sense of exclusive political power. We cannot know until we try.

It does seem, in sum, as if one of the options we have not yet tried in South Vietnam is to let those who live there decide their future for themselves.

IV

At breakfast on January 5 we were told that we would see Prime Minister Pham Van Dong two hours later. We had not expected the meeting until our last day in the country, January 6.

At the appointed hour we were driven to the spacious flower-surrounded executive residence. Herbert recorded his account of the visit: "The Prime Minister, unaccompanied, hurried down several stone steps and greeted us. He shook hands vigorously and invited us into a large and comfortable room. About his throat was a scarf; he looks all of his sixty years. Rather dark-complexioned, slightly above the average height here, a very high forehead, serious eyes. . . After inquiring about our health and expressing concern lest our trip cause us difficulties upon returning home, he rather quickly began talking about the urgent questions facing his—and our—country and therefore the world."[4]

The text of our interview is not official, although Tom checked it carefully with the interpreter afterward. At supper-time January 5 we received long-awaited written answers to the written questions we had submitted to Prime Minister Pham Van Dong through the Peace Committee a week earlier. Both texts follow:

THE INTERVIEW

The Prime Minister. We are a people of good will. We need many people to understand us. Especially do we need the people of good will in America to understand us. If we understand each other more fully it is a good thing. Your visit marks a new step.

In fact you as well as we are facing a difficult situation. In

[4] *Mission to Hanoi* (New York, 1966), p. 60.

this situation you and we have to recognize what is the biggest problem. What is the underlying cause and immediate reason for the war in Vietnam? Only when we return to these can anything be settled. Diplomatic maneuvers and tricks cannot settle the question. If they are good enough they can deceive people for a time. When people understand they have been deceived, it will be bad for those who deceived them.

The Vietnamese people feel they are fighting for a just cause against barbarous aggression. That is the central reality. The same thing happened when you fought against the British. It is very simple. We are very strong, and the longer we fight the stronger we become. When we started fighting against the French we did not know how it would end. This time the people of South Vietnam are doing the same thing. It is more difficult to fight against the United States aggressors, but the liberation movement in South Vietnam has become stronger than we here expected. I personally could not have imagined it.

I was very anxious and concerned about what would happen when two hundred thousand American troops came. But the liberation movement has been able to fight them on every battlefield, even in the military bases, even in Saigon. The strength of the people is endless. We cannot predict everything beforehand. The aggressors can defeat an army but they cannot defeat a people determined to win independence. When we say that we will fight ten or twenty years longer this is not beautiful words, not rhetoric. Even the children are ready. This too has made me think hard. If we do not succeed, later generations will continue.

It is not true that we do not desire peace. We desire it more than anybody. The war is happening in our country and killing our people. This building might be destroyed and that would be a loss. But our grief is about the children, the women, the old and young people who are killed. We feel pain in our heart because of these sufferings. Surely we desire peace more than President Johnson. But peace at what cost? All the problems lie here. We must have independence. We would rather die than be enslaved. There is often reference to United States honor. But what about our honor? And what is the true honor of the United States?

We take this occasion to say that there is no hatred between the people of the United States and the people of Vietnam. We respect the American people. We respect the history of struggle of the American people. We believe the light of truth will win us the support of the American people.

Question. Since December twentieth when President Johnson said he would "knock at any door," has the United States attempted to make direct contact with the D.R.V.?

Answer. No.

Question. Do you mean that no D.R.V. ambassador anywhere in the world has been contacted by the United States, as well as that there has been no direct communication with Hanoi?

Answer. In that broader sense of the question, the answer is still No.

Question. What concrete actions would the United States need to take to convince you of its sincere desire to make peace?

Answer. I am not the United States Government. The problem is simple. We know there are very complex questions, but the beginning must be simple. If the United States really wants peace, everything complicated can be settled. We know this, because in fighting you get to know your opponent. The peace offensive is intended to deceive third parties. But we are not deceived.

The essence of the United States peace offensive is the idea of negotiation from strength. There is nothing new in it. Absolutely nothing new. What is the reason for the peace offensive? To win public opinion, particularly American public opinion. Only by so doing can President Johnson escalate the war. It is clear that he has prepared expansion of the war. It is also clear that he has not recognized the four-point program of the D.R.V. as a basis for negotiation.

The world is one. It is becoming smaller and smaller. History makes us closer to each other. That is a tendency which nothing can prevent. The United States aggressors are going against history. In spite of their economic and military strength, in spite of tricks and maneuvers, they will fail. The great truth of our time is that we must be brothers, fraternal toward each other. That is a noble ideology. If you have the opportunity to meet President Johnson, will you please ask him: Why is he fighting against us? There is no reason for it. If the United States accepts the Four Points sincerely, and proves its sincerity by the actions it thinks necessary, this can bring honor to the United States. The war cannot be honorable for it. Continuing the war means killing plain people, ordinary people.

At some point the United States will have to want peace. At present it does not. We hope that time will come soon. But it is not up to us to decide. As for us, as long as the United States aggressors are in our country we must continue to fight.

Ask the people in the streets. A five-year-old boy will tell you that he will continue to fight. This is not because he is bellicose. It is not easy for a foreigner to understand this situation. We have been fighting for decades for our independence.

Nobody wants war. But we must have independence. The highest sentiment is fraternity. This age is the age of that sentiment. That is why it is clear the United States war of aggression will be defeated.

THE WRITTEN
QUESTIONS AND ANSWERS

Question. What is your comment on the idea that the Democratic Republic of Vietnam and the National Liberation Front refuse all offers to negotiate? Is it not the case that the D.R.V. and the N.L.F. set conditions for negotiations? What must the United States do before there can be negotiations?

Answer. I am not going to answer in the place of the South Vietnam National Front for Liberation.

As far as the Government of the D.R.V. is concerned, may I quote a few sentences from the January 4, 1966, statement of our Foreign Ministry. These sentences are:

"It is the unswerving stand of the Government of the D.R.V. to strictly respect the 1954 Geneva Agreements on Vietnam, and to correctly implement their basic provisions . . .

"A political settlement of the Vietnam problem can be envisaged only when the U.S. Government has accepted the four-point stand of the Government of the D.R.V., has proved this by actual deeds, at the same time has stopped unconditionally and for good its air raids and all other acts of war against the D.R.V."

Question. What is the meaning of the third point of Prime Minister Pham Van Dong, "the internal affairs of South Vietnam must be settled by the South Vietnamese people themselves, in accordance with the program of the N.L.F."?

Answer. The third point is a very important one in the four-point stand of the Government of the D.R.V. from which it can by no means be dissociated. The U.S. authorities have recently stated that they do not accept this point. Thus they recognize neither the sacred right to self-determination of the people of South Vietnam, nor the National Front for Liberation, the sole genuine representative of the people of South Vietnam. In short, they do not accept the four-point stand of the Government of the D.R.V., which means they are still pursuing a policy of aggression in South Vietnam.

Question. If the United States withdraws its troops, would the D.R.V. withdraw its troops from South Vietnam?

Answer. The so-called "presence of the forces of the D.R.V. in South Vietnam" is a sheer U.S. fabrication in order to justify their war of aggression in South Vietnam.

Question. Exactly how would the creation of a national coalition government in South Vietnam and the eventual reunification of South with North Vietnam come about?

Answer. The setting up of a national coalition government in South Vietnam is an internal affair of the people of South Vietnam. It is to be settled by the people of South Vietnam in accordance with the program of the N.L.F. This program provides for the establishment of "a broad national democratic coalition administration including representatives of all strata of people, nationalities, political parties, religious communities, and patriotic personalities. We must wrest back the people's economic, political, social, and cultural interests, realize independence and democracy, improve the people's living conditions, carry out a policy of peace and neutrality, and advance toward peaceful reunification of the Fatherland."

The reunification of Vietnam is an internal affair of the Vietnamese people, it is to be settled by the Vietnamese people in the two zones. On this subject, it is said in the program of the N.L.F.:

"The urgent demand of our people throughout the country is to reunify the Fatherland by peaceful means. The N.L.F. undertakes the gradual reunification of the country by peaceful means, on the principle of negotiations and discussions between the two zones on all forms and measures beneficial to the Vietnamese people and Fatherland."

And the program of the Vietnam Fatherland Front reads in part:

"To achieve in favorable conditions the peaceful reunification of our Fatherland, we must take into account the real situation in the two zones, the interests and legitimate aspirations of all sections of the population. At the same time, we must conduct negotiations to arrange the holding of free general elections in order to achieve national unity without either side trying to exert pressure on, or trying to annex the other."

Question. Would the Geneva Conference be reconvened?

Answer. In reply to this question, I would like to quote a sentence from the April 8, 1965, statement of the Government of the D.R.V. about our four-point stand: "If this basis is accepted, favorable conditions will be created for the peaceful settlement of the Vietnam problem, and it will be possible to consider the reconvening of an international conference of the 1954 Geneva Conference on Vietnam."

Question. It is often said by the United States Government that the N.L.F. is an agent of the D.R.V. and that the D.R.V. is controlled by the Chinese People's Republic. What is your reply?

Answer. This is a vile fabrication designed to slander the Vietnamese people, the N.L.F., the D.R.V., and the P.R.C. [People's Republic of China].

The N.L.F. is the sole genuine representative of the people of South Vietnam, it enjoys great prestige among the people of South Vietnam and in the world, it is now leading the infinitely heroic and certain to be victorious fight waged by the people of South Vietnam against U.S. imperialist aggression.

The U.S. refusal to recognize the N.L.F. shows all the more clearly that the U.S. Government is bent on pursuing the war of aggression in South Vietnam; consequently, it will sustain even heavier defeats.

The D.R.V. is a socialist, independent, and sovereign country. Its relations with the brotherly P.R.C. are founded on the principle of mutual equality, cooperation, and mutual aid. These are relations between comrades-in-arms, as close with each other as lips and teeth.

V

Two statements which Pham Van Dong made to us have occasioned great controversy in the United States. The first was that there were no North Vietnamese troops in South Vietnam; the second, that the United States Government had not communicated with the Government of North Vietnam from the beginning of the peace offensive up to the day on which we spoke with the Prime Minister, i.e., December 20, 1965, to January 5, 1966. This is the time to say a little more about each.

Just what is meant by North Vietnamese troops? Bernard Fall estimated that eighty thousand Vietminh soldiers regrouped to the North after the Geneva Agreements. The Mansfield Report stated that in the fall of 1965 there were fourteen thousand North Vietnamese soldiers in South Vietnam. We would like to suggest that persons who have traveled from North to South to fight against the Saigon–U.S. forces may have been Southerners returning to their homes and not regular units of the D.R.V. Army. If so, Prime Minister Pham Van Dong's statement that "the so-called 'presence of the forces of the D.R.V. in South Vietnam' is a sheer U.S. fabrication" would be technically correct.

The State Department's White Paper of February 27, 1965, declared that "as many as 75 percent of the more than 4,400 Vietcong who are known to have entered the South in the first eight months of 1964 were natives of North Vietnam." I. F. Stone subjected this affirmation to a devastating critique:

. . . a careful reading of the text and the appendices turns up the names of only six North Vietnamese infiltrees. In Part I of the White Paper, Section B gives "individual case histories of North Vietnamese soldiers" sent South by Hanoi but all nine of these are of South Vietnamese origin. The next Section, C, is headed "Infiltration of Native North Vietnamese." It names five infiltrees but one of these is also from the South. That leaves four North Vietnamese natives. Then, in Appendix C, we are given the case histories and photographs of nine other Vietcong sent South by Hanoi. The report does not explain which ones were originally from the South but it does give the names of the provinces in which they were born. When these are checked, it turns out that only two of the nine were born in North Vietnam. This gives us a total of six Northern infiltrees. It is strange that after five years of fighting, the White Paper can cite so few.[5]

D.R.V. and N.L.F. statements indicate that a substantial repatriation of Southerners from the North may have occurred, but not until after American escalation in February, 1965. On March 22, 1965, the N.L.F. Central Committee asserted:

While the U.S. imperialists are constantly sowing sufferings and death in South Vietnam, the South Vietnam National Liberation Front, if need be, cannot but call back the sons and

[5] "A Reply to the White Paper," *Vietnam*, ed. Gettleman, pp. 320–321.

daughters of South Vietnam, who have regrouped to the North in observance of the cease-fire agreement and who had to live far from South Vietnam during ten long years, to take arms to annihilate the enemy to save their country and families.

This statement was soon after echoed by the North. On March 27, 1965, the North Vietnamese Fatherland Front declared over Radio Hanoi (as monitored by the United States):

The struggle of the people in the two zones against U.S. imperialism is being more closely coordinated than ever before. The Presidium and Secretariat of the VFF Central Committee fully approve and warmly support the stand of the N.L.F.S.V. in calling back, if need be, the sons and daughters of South Vietnam who have regrouped to the North in observance of the cease-fire agreement to take arms to annihilate the enemy.

The next day *Nhan Dan*, organ of the North Vietnamese Communist Party, said:

There is a large number of South Vietnamese people regrouped to the north under the Geneva agreements. . . . In observance of the cease-fire agreement, they have had to live far from South Vietnam for 10 long years. In the face of the crimes committed by the U.S. imperialists and their flunkeys in their native villages, every one of them is seething with wrath and nurturing the determination to wipe out the enemy and save his country. Many have had the opportunity to show that determination during the valiant fights to annihilate the enemy air and naval forces which attacked the north. Now, learning that the N.L.F.S.V. has declared that, if need be, it will call them back to take arms to annihilate the enemy to save their country and families, every one of them is feeling aroused and is eager to fulfill all *new tasks required by the new situation* [authors' italics].

Predictably, no doubt, a Radio Hanoi broadcast monitored the next day (March 29) reported that a meeting of "over six hundred representatives of South Vietnamese army men, public servants, and other people regrouped to the north under the 1954 Geneva Agreements held a meeting here last night to voice warm support for the 22 March 1965 statement of the N.L.F.S.V. and the 27 March 1965 statement of the Vietnam Fatherland Front." In particular they expressed their readiness "to return to their native places in the south to take up arms and fight the U.S. aggressors and their lackeys."

The N.L.F. as late as August 3, 1965, issued a statement in response to Lyndon Johnson's July 28 press conference, declaring: "We call on our South Vietnamese compatriots and armymen who regrouped in the North to quickly organize their ranks and get ready to return to the South when they are ordered to in order to fight the U.S. aggressors and save the country and their families."

We suspect that the much-celebrated aggression from the North in fact amounts to the return, after the escalation of February, 1965, of several thousand Vietminh soldiers who had regrouped to the North under the Geneva Agreements.[6]

VI

The second question—whether or not the United States made contact with the Government of North Vietnam during the peace offensive—does not seem to involve any problem of definition. After the Prime Minister told us that there had been no contact, Staughton (as the text of the interview

---

[6] This hypothesis also is advanced by Burchett in his *Vietnam North* (pp. 126 ff.), which International Publishers kindly permitted us to read in page proofs as we were reading the proofs of this book.

shows) asked if this meant that there had been no contact through North Vietnamese embassies as well as directly to Hanoi. Again the Prime Minister answered No. If Presidential Press Secretary Bill D. Moyers was correct in his subsequent statement that a message was passed from a United States official to a North Vietnamese official before January 5, apparently in Rangoon, the North Vietnamese Prime Minister clearly told us a diplomatic untruth.

But even assuming that Moyers was correct and Pham Van Dong untruthful, there would be not the slightest basis for interpreting the incident as one more illustration of the other side's intransigence. The fact that the other side assesses American intentions more by what we do than by what we say means that whether or not the United States sent a note to North Vietnam at Christmastime, and almost regardless of that putative note's contents, no progress was possible toward peace unless the United States war effort was significantly de-escalated.

This approach to Johnsonian rhetoric did not begin in December, 1965. It was also the criterion applied by the other side to the Johns Hopkins speech of April. On April 11, 1965, the Hanoi newspaper *Nhan Dan* stated: "Eisenhower, Kennedy and then Johnson have untiringly talked of peace to the Vietnamese people as well as the world people. Also in the same period, the U.S. imperialists in South Vietnam have wire-pulled their henchmen and together with them killed nearly 170,000 persons, wounded or tortured to invalidity nearly 800,000, and detained some 400,000 in more than 1,000 jails." Turning to the Johns Hopkins speech specifically, the paper continued:

On 9 April 1965, just over 24 hours after U.S. President Johnson boasted about his desire for peace at Johns Hopkins

University, U.S. aircraft again bombed and strafed North Vietnam. Meanwhile, the U.S. Embassy in Saigon openly announced the introduction into South Vietnam of more U.S. Marine battalions and one squadron of U.S. jet fighters. On the same day, U.S. aircraft encroached upon China's airspace over Hainan Island, and when attacked by Chinese planes, they fled away in panic.

"He whets his knife while telling his beads" is the traditional trick of the imperialists, with Johnson taking the lead.

A week later (April 19) the English-language Radio Hanoi said: "Since 7 April 1965, the U.S. imperialists have introduced into South Vietnam two more battalions of U.S. Marines totaling three thousand men. . . . It is clear that Johnson's speech is but a smokescreen to cover up the U.S. imperialists' new military adventures in Vietnam." Meantime the N.L.F. Presidium had met on April 15 and made the same evaluation: "Johnson's proposal was used as a smokescreen, because behind this smoke thousands of U.S. Marines and troops were landed in South Vietnam, the barbarous military operations have not been discontinued in South Vietnam, the airstrikes including night airstrikes have not been suspended in North Vietnam, and so forth."

This then was the background for Hanoi's response to the United States note which accompanied the five-day bombing pause in May, 1965:

. . . the U.S. imperialists' deeds never match with their words. In the period of the so-called suspension of the bombings over North Vietnam from 12 to 17 May this year, U.S. aircraft and warships continued to encroach upon the territorial waters of the D.R.V. for spying, provocative and raiding activities. Two U.S. F-105 jetfighters were downed over Nghe on 13 and 17 May respectively. Meanwhile, the U.S. brought to South Vietnam [words unclear] more combat troops and the U.S.-puppets intensified their ground and air raids against the population. On 14 May alone, U.S. puppet aircraft flew 186 sorties.[7]

And this, too, was the other side's response to the Christmas peace offensive.

Our conversations in North Vietnam made clear that Hanoi reacted to the bombing pause and the peace offensive with the implicit question: Is there anything in all of this to suggest an American decision to withdraw? Hanoi answered this question, No. On our return to the United States January 9, we summarized the North Vietnamese view as follows: "As seen from Hanoi, there is a deep inconsistency in United States policy between the peaceful posture looking toward a negotiated settlement, and the interventionist posture which has in view the permanent partition of Vietnam and an expanded war. This two-sidedness makes the policy seem suspect and hypocritical to the Vietnamese, who hear overtures of peace but also pledges to stay in Vietnam; who know of the pause in bombing but experience a daily military buildup in the South."

Basing ourselves on a statement by Voice of Vietnam Radio on December 30, authoritative articles in *Nhan Dan* for December 31 and January 3, the statement by the D.R.V. Foreign Ministry on January 4, and our January 5 conversation with the Prime Minister, we continued: "For those to whom we talked in Vietnam, the record of events in recent weeks proves clearly the continuing inconsistency of American policy. . . . To be sure, there is now a pause in the bombing of North Vietnam. But the Vietnamese remind one that the last pause was followed immediately by expansion of the war. During the current pause, while the United States has been waiting for a so-called signal from Hanoi, Vietnamese sources have been emphasizing that President Johnson's words are accompanied

[7] *I. F. Stone's Weekly,* December 20, 1965.

by new escalation in the South. According to these sources, the day after President Johnson spoke of knocking on any door the Department of Defense admitted the use of toxic chemicals and authorized 'hot pursuit' by American troops into Cambodia. A week later, when President Johnson announced his fourteen points, four thousand new American troops of the Twenty-fifth Division arrived at Pleiku and B-52 bombers flew 322 sorties over South Vietnam. Hanoi sources also point to the arrival in Saigon between December 21 and January 1 of the Chief of Staff of the United States Army, the chairman of the Joint Chiefs of Staff, the Secretary of the Army, and the Secretary of the Air Force. Past experience suggests to them that such conferences immediately precede new escalation."

Prime Minister Pham Van Dong referred to these and other acts of American escalation during the Christmas peace offensive in his speech on January 8 to welcome Aleksandr Shelepin, a member of the Soviet Communist Party Presidium and Secretariat, who led a high-ranking Soviet delegation to visit North Vietnam. Asking what is for the other side the crucial question, he began: "Do the Americans' deeds square with their professed desire for peace?" The Prime Minister answered his own question this way:

Not at all. . . . American "peace" speeches are followed by moves escalating the war. The United States is pouring more troops into South Vietnam and conducting large-scale punitive operations, using strategic aircraft to bomb densely populated areas and destroying numerous villages. More and more it is using chemicals and poison gas for the massive destruction of civilians and crops. Not long ago a large group of American generals arrived in Saigon to discuss measures for expanding "aid" to the puppets and the war of aggression. In North Vietnam, U.S. aircraft daily carry out training flights along the coast and reconnaissance flights in preparation for new raids. In addition, the U.S. imperialists are stepping up air raids on the liberated regions of Laos and brazenly discuss plans for invading Central and South Laos and Cambodia.[8]

The day after the D.R.V. Foreign Ministry statement of January 4 the N.L.F. Central Committee made a declaration which followed its predecessor in stressing the contrast between American deeds and American words. "The more the U.S. imperialists prattle about 'peace negotiation,' the more feverishly they step up and expand the war," the Front asserted. The N.L.F. statement laid particular stress on the expansion of chemical warfare coincidentally with the peace offensive. It said:

. . . from December 7 to 14, 1965, while prattling about "peace negotiation," the US imperialists carried out massive poison sprays, notably in Ben Tre province, where 46,000 persons were affected, mostly women—including expecting mothers—aged people and children, tens of thousands of hectares of rice and other crops were destroyed, and a great number of domestic animals killed.

Only deeds, not words, could convince the Front of a genuine American desire for peace. The statement said:

. . . if they sincerely desire peace, they must prove it by practical deeds, namely to stop all ground operations as well as air raids against the South Vietnamese people, to withdraw all their troops from South Vietnam, to dismantle all military bases, to stop definitively and unconditionally all air raids on the Democratic Republic of Vietnam, to respect the 1954 Geneva Agreements, and to let the South Vietnamese people settle their internal affairs by themselves.

[8] The text of this speech is reprinted in Aptheker, *Mission to Hanoi*, pp. 114–120.

The other side's evaluation of the peace offensive was shared by so hardbeaked an American hawk as journalist Joseph Alsop. Writing for the New York *Herald Tribune* of February 28, 1966, Alsop said that the cause of the peace offensive was the "panic" of Washington when it decided in November, 1965, that American troops in Vietnam would have to be substantially increased. The panic, said Alsop, concerned the political consequences of such further escalation:

> The first consequence of the panic was the peace offensive and the pause. . . . One must assume that domestic political considerations were the prime motives of the vast international vaudeville which the President staged.

We have seen no reason to revise that conclusion.[9]

[9] Hanoi and Haiphong were bombed after this chapter was written. A group of distinguished American scholars concluded that French and Canadian diplomats had made important progress toward a negotiated settlement and that the bombing was timed "to make certain that Hanoi would once again go back to its hard attitude." (Franz Schurmann, *et al.*, *The Politics of Escalation in Vietnam* [Greenwich, Conn., 1966], p. 139). This conclusion is supported by the fact that when Staughton met Do Xuan Oanh and other North Vietnamese in Geneva the week before the bombing, they were keenly excited about the possibility of negotiations, quite in contrast to their attitude at Christmastime.

By fall, 1966, the *New York Times* in an editorial called on the Johnson Administration for "actual de-escalation" (September 28) as well as verbal peace offensives, and President Charles De Gaulle in his September 1 speech at Phnom Penh stated—in agreement with the argument of this chapter—that the key to peace was "the decision and the commitment" of the United States to withdraw.

8

PEACE NEGOTIATIONS II:
RUSSIA AND CHINA

I

Clearly the other side's approach to peace involves the attitudes of China and the Soviet Union, the two great allies of the D.R.V. and N.L.F.

We saw nothing in Hanoi to suggest a struggle of "pro-Moscow" and "pro-Peking" factions. That struggle may be going on but what was said to us was always: we appreciate the help of our Russian friends, we appreciate the help of our Chinese friends, but we make our own decisions. These sentiments are coupled with a desire to be nationally independent of all the Great Powers. This was conveyed to us in our discussions with every Vietnamese. In a July, 1966, interview given to Burchett, one North Vietnamese official put it in this typical way:

Our present struggle was imposed on us by the Americans, not because of any ideological line from outside. The existence of the socialist camp of which we are now part is a powerful support for us. But whether Peking or Moscow existed or not, whether the socialist camp existed or not, we would have no choice but to take up arms and fight, as our ancestors have always done for national salvation.[1]

One thing about which we feel certain, despite the brevity of our trip, is the depth of Vietnamese desire to be independent of China. Herbert and Staughton visited a museum of Vietnamese history (different from the Museum of the Vietnamese Revolution which the three of us visited together) where the most cherished exhibit was wooden stakes that had been driven into the bed of the river between Haiphong and Hanoi to stave in the Chinese junks invading in the fifteenth century.

Our other strongest impression concerning the possible relationship among Moscow, Peking, and Hanoi is that the Vietnamese experience of revolution is much closer to the Chinese than to the Russian. For the present generation of Russians, "revolution" has meant the monumental labor of building the world's first planned industrial economy. War seems to the Russians as to North Americans a catastrophic intrusion of disaster into everyday life, a "plague" in the sense Camus portrayed the Nazi occupation of Europe. When the Russians think of war, they think of 1941–45 when twenty million Soviet citizens were killed, and they want it never to happen again.

For both the Chinese and Vietnamese, in contrast, everything they have achieved has come through war: international war, which set the capitalist powers at odds and gave Asian revolutionaries their chance; civil war, which enveloped the Chinese from 1924 to 1949 and has now lasted in Vietnam a

[1] *National Guardian*, July 16, 1966.

similar quarter-century. It is a caricature to argue that this experience makes Chinese and Vietnamese "bellicose." What it means is that the revolutionary learns to fight with one hand and build a new society with the other, to break through Camus' distinction between the "rebel" interested in present positive action and the "revolutionary" concerned with distant visions, and to be both at once. War will appear to such a man not as a looming catastrophe but as the medium of the only daily life he has known.

There were dozens of indications of this attitude among Chinese and Vietnamese to whom we talked. Remember, said the N.L.F. representative in Moscow, that in most of the "liberated areas" there is peace and the work of building a new society goes forward. In both Peking and Hanoi, we solemnly were told that if America felt driven to use nuclear weapons and if every Chinese or Vietnamese were killed, then the revolutionary impulse would go on elsewhere. Tang Ming-chao said: "The world will go on. There will be other revolutionary forces. I spoke recently to Japanese young people and told them there is a danger of Chinese revisionism. I told them to grow up and fight the danger of Chinese revisionism."

Another way to express what binds together Chinese and Vietnamese (and Cuban, and—ironically—Yugoslavian) revolutionary experiences is that each movement came to power through guerrilla war. Guerrilla war means, to begin with, that in the process of taking over the state one creates a replica of the larger society one hopes to build in the microcosm of a remote rural "base": a Yenan or a Sierra Maestra. Just as the European middle-class rehearsed the reality of bourgeois society in the free cities of the Middle Ages, so the twentieth-century guerrilla finds himself forced by circumstance to live out even before the "first stage" of socialist construction many relationships which Marxist theory prescribes only for the Communist "final stage": equality of income (food is scarce, and everyone eats from the same pot); a blending of manual and intellectual labor (Mao kept a garden in Yenan); an emphasis upon the power of human will to overcome objective difficulties.

The guerrilla experience was apparent in the frequent references of Hanoi informants to what happened "in the Resistance" or "in the jungle." It was equally obvious when Tang Ming-chao used, to describe China's anticipation of an American invasion, the same words which, as we saw in the Museum of the Chinese Revolution, Mao had used to dismiss Chiang's counterrevolutionary columns in the nineteen-thirties: "Let him come, let him take all the pots and pans, we will defeat him anyway."

Russians refer to their great struggle against the Germans as their "patriotic war." Chinese and Vietnamese use a likesounding phrase, "people's war," but mean something different by it. The essence of people's war is that it does not overcome by material means, such as the Soviet tanks which rolled the Germans westward, or by superior manpower. It succeeds by combining political and military techniques: by creating higher morale among the partisans (one thinks of N.L.F. defectors, as reported in the *New York Times*, saying that in the Army of the Front soldiers are punished by being sent to the rear); and by undermining the morale of the antagonist. Concretely, what we are calling a Russian conception of the war in Vietnam would lead to the conclusion that America's military resources are greater than those of the French and hence the Front may not lose, but cannot win; while the Chinese-Vietnamese view lays stress upon the political "contradictions" embodied in the American cause: between the American Government and world public opinion (above all, if nuclear weapons are used), between the American Government and the American people (as draft calls increase), and between the American Government and the Saigon Government (since, as they see it, every American soldier who lands in South Vietnam convinces one more South Vietnamese neutralist that Saigon is an American puppet).

Finally, of course, guerrilla war requires a readiness to die. Norman Morrison and Nguyen Van Troi are held up as models to Vietnamese young people. Similarly Tang Ming-chao's daughter told us that she and her fellows studied four case histories in order to decide proper behavior. Two were young men who put personal advancement ahead of the welfare of the community. Case history three was that of a young man who died accidentally and whose diary, found on his body, revealed the many things he had done for others without ever making mention of it. Case history four was that of a soldier who threw himself on a mine to save the lives of his comrades, whose diary included the phrases: "Not afraid of hardships, not afraid of death."

The West is seen, both in China and Vietnam, as lacking such hardihood. A Vietnamese remarked that Russians "drink too much"; another observed that no doubt Americans would find difficult Vietnamese "white nights" (nights without sleep). We have said nothing about the question of color because not once in our journey was the Chinese or Vietnamese sense of injustice described in racial terms. Yet, clearly the picture of the white man—Russian or American—as "soft" verges on a racial stereotype. (Tom thought that our hosts' neglect of the issue stemmed partly from politeness and partly from the Marxist conviction that bourgeois Americans, despite their color, can be pressured to withdraw from a futile colonial war.) Racial considerations are raised frequently by Asian diplomats. For instance, Cambodia's Foreign Minister, Huot

Sambath, asked the United Nations General Assembly on October 17, 1966, whether the U.S. would ever use against white people the kind of violence employed every day in Vietnam.

In summary, then, our approach to the Sino-Soviet split rejects the common American emphasis on great power rivalry. We find equally unhelpful the concern of both Russians and Chinese to articulate their differences from the standpoint of Marxist theory, political "betrayal," and historical "correctness." To us the split appears to spring from certain paradoxical consequences of the fact that socialism first came to power in a single, underdeveloped, and predominantly white country. The origin of the controversy lies in a variety of revolutionary experiences.

II

If the Sino-Soviet split is not evident in Vietnam, it is made plain for every traveler in China. In each airport we visited (Peking, Wuhan, Nanning) there was a literature rack with booklets, in many languages, analyzing the dispute and attacking the Soviet Union.

We discussed with members of the Chinese Peace Committee what the Chinese call "the U.S.–Soviet collaboration to dominate the world." The Chinese thesis is that the Soviet Union has defined its interests to be more in harmony with those of the United States than with the interests of the revolutionary movements of the world. The Soviet Union, it is argued, has decided that its greatest benefit lies in opening up East-West trade while diminishing the cost of a dangerous nuclear arms race. The Chinese say that they, in contrast, see imperialism and national independence struggles as more important realities than the arms race or peace among the affluent countries.

Tang Ming-chao told us that the Chinese "have warm feelings for the Soviet Union, and we are afraid they are going to be hurt since it is unrealistic to expect that the U.S. wants to share its domination of the world." "The Soviets are soft, and when you are soft," he warned, "a disease can develop." Not softness so much as weariness of war might be the Russian motivation, we thought, and asked whether or not Tang agreed.

His answer was stiff. "Some quit after torture, some get stronger." He warned: "Water always goes to the lowest place: our morale is strong, but when your morale has softened, your weapons get soft. We would not be displeased if the Soviet Union does not come to our aid if we are attacked. But if the Soviet Union is attacked, and a world war begins, we will come to its aid."

Tang Ming-chao described the genesis of the Sino-Soviet split as follows: "After Camp David, in 1959, Khrushchev said we should give up Taiwan and give in to Nehru. We wondered about this. We had wondered about his 1956 speech. Stalin was a world leader, but we were not consulted in advance about Khrushchev's speech. We thought his evaluation of Stalin was wrong, and we did not care for such criticism of a man who was dead and could not defend himself. We also thought that Khrushchev should have practiced self-criticism since he was present during the Stalin period.

"In 1958, we had refused when Khrushchev proposed a joint fleet in the Pacific under Soviet control. We told him we did not need his protection. 'What would you do in a war?,' he asked. We said we could go into the mountains and fight guerrilla warfare.

"This became the biggest question since liberation. We had three choices: one, to follow the Soviets, occupy the second chair in the movement—then we would become revisionist; two, to keep quiet, and continue to get aid and technicians—but this would have confused our people; three, to speak up and let him crack down. It took us until 1960 to decide. Now we will stick to it."

On the question of nuclear war, a principal bone of contention between the Chinese and the Soviets, Tang said: "All weapons should be banned and destroyed. To begin with we must reach an agreement not to use them. The atmospheric test ban was really nothing but a way to keep a Soviet-American monopoly. The effect of fallout is exaggerated. The worst thing is the nuclear monopoly, the blackmail and the gambling. Cuba was a case of nuclear gambling by the Soviets. They were thinking more of the United States than of Cuba. They had no business putting nuclear weapons in Cuba. We were not even consulted, yet we are bound by treaty to aid them in war. You should rely on people, not on nuclear weapons. We thought Khrushchev was wrong in saying he would use the weapons. Where? Havana? New York?"

As for Vietnam, the Chinese claim the Russians only feign support in order to achieve a position of strength from which to urge a cease-fire and negotiations. They contend that under Khrushchev the Soviet Union favored a general "disengagement" of military forces in Indochina, the Soviet motive being that of a great power fearing war over a smaller country. As the war developed, the Soviets switched to a policy of direct support. The Chinese think, however, that Soviet support is motivated by a desire to keep the war limited. In the Chinese view, the Russians are allying with the Indians and Japanese to "contain" China, the price being an abortion of the revolution in Vietnam and settlement of the war short of Hanoi's objectives.

III

What truth is there in these Chinese contentions about Soviet policy toward Vietnam? We cannot judge the present controversy about military aid. (In the Hanoi factory we visited, 60 percent of the machines were said to be imported, from France, Czechoslovakia, and the Soviet Union. Announced Soviet aid to Hanoi, which rose "sharply since the United States began bombing North Vietnam early in 1965," includes military equipment, industrial machinery, power generating and road building equipment.[2]) As to the past, the record as we piece it together shows a strong Chinese case, with two major exceptions: 1. Ho generally is thought to have followed a "Soviet line," as in the negotiations of 1945–46 and 1954; 2. the Chinese themselves supported the Soviet approach at the time of the Geneva Agreements.

Throughout the late thirties and the forties the Soviets tended to counsel that the Vietnamese subordinate their demands for independence to the needs of the French Communists who, it was expected, would come to power in France and peacefully release the Vietnamese from the colonial framework. As it developed, the Popular Front did come to power, though the Communist Party did not, but the Front failed to end colonial policies. Ho remained patient, apparently against pressure from the Trotskyists and others within his own Party, and made the risky decision to seek a postwar role for Vietnam within the French Union. During negotiations in

[2] *New York Times,* September 26, 1966.

Paris with the French, Ho was quoted as saying: "While we want to govern ourselves . . . I need your professional men, your engineers, and your capital to build a strong and independent Vietnam."[3] This statement was made in 1946; the previous year, in November, Ho had accepted the Russian-French suggestion of dissolving the Communist Party. The result was that the British entered South Vietnam, helped to rearm the French, attacked Vietminh officials who were governing the country, and civil war resumed. Ho spent a year in Europe trying unsuccessfully to negotiate with the French but returned with virtually nothing to face his critics in Vietnam.

At the Geneva Conference, Gettleman summarized, the Soviets and the Chinese who were allied with them at the time "actually put pressure on the Vietminh to accept far less territory than they had liberated by force of arms, and to drop claims on Cambodia and Laos."[4]

Some of the details are in Lancaster's book.[5] The situation in 1953 was this. In September, Ho was still speaking of "victory" as a precondition of peace talks, and the French Government was deeply divided about continuing the war. The Prime Minister, Joseph Laniel, and the Foreign Minister, Georges Bidault, were intent on avoiding negotiations until the French military position was stronger; they had just received 385 million dollars from Eisenhower for Indochina over and above the 400 million dollars in U.S. aid already sent for fiscal 1953–54. On the other hand, Pierre Mendes-France and others in the National Assembly were strongly convinced that broadened military commitments would eliminate the chance for a negotiated settlement. A majority of delegates in the Assembly

---

[3] Robert Shaplen, *The Lost Revolution* (New York, 1965), p. 43.
[4] *Vietnam*, ed. Gettleman, p. 116.
[5] *The Emancipation of French Indochina*, Chapters XV–XVII.

favored negotiated withdrawal and were divided only on the manner.

Ho apparently decided to influence the French political balance of power by an interview published on November 29 in the Stockholm paper *Expressen* in which he declared willingness to examine any French proposals, stressing too that the French would have to recognize the independence of Vietnam. This gesture undercut Laniel who had been claiming that Ho was unwilling to discuss a settlement.

The Soviets also intervened in November of that year, with a suggestion to the French that a conference might be convened to include the question of Indochina. But the Russians' interest was in influencing the debate within the French Assembly about whether or not France should join the proposed European Defense Community. The EDC had been conceived at a Paris conference the previous year, and would have involved the Americans deeply in joint defense activity with European countries, contrary to the Soviet hope that Europe could be unified on a basis independent of the U.S. V. M. Molotov was proposing, in effect, that France refuse to join the EDC in exchange for which the Soviets would arrange a settlement in Indochina. Bidault, in response to public pressure, agreed in February to come to a Geneva meeting in April, and he deferred all moves to ratify the EDC plan in the Assembly although stating that he had no intention of selling out the EDC.

These moves, reported Lancaster, "appear to have dismayed" the Vietminh who thought more headway should be made in the war prior to negotiations. The announcement of the Geneva meeting, Lancaster said, was one of the reasons for the Vietminh decision to bear down on the French garrison at Dienbienphu. This was especially the view of General Vo

Nguyen Giap, and it is said that the Chinese Communists agreed with and physically supported the plan although they also had agreed with the Soviet proposal for the Geneva Conference (apparently because of the legitimacy it would give them).

On May 8 the conference finally began in Geneva, one day after the Vietminh victory at Dienbienphu. In the meantime, there had been a new development which taxed the Soviet Union's diplomatic ingenuity: a Dulles threat to use American nuclear weapons on Dienbienphu, with support from French generals and officials, had been averted. The British had allied with the Soviets in the view that such a move would possibly lead to world war, and the U.S. was persuaded not to undertake the bombing because of this division within the West, and because of the apprehension of U.S. congressmen and senators. The Soviets thought, and still think, that their strategy probably prevented terrible destruction of an unprecedented kind in Vietnam. Lancaster said that Anthony Eden was impressed with, and reinforced by, Molotov's "conciliatory attitude."

The Vietminh were not so conciliatory in Eden's eyes, however. Pham Van Dong came to Geneva denouncing the French and demanding: recognition of Vietnamese national independence and sovereignty; the same for the Khmers and Pathet Lao; withdrawal of all foreign troops from Indochina; free elections, conducted by local committees, in all these areas. Dong expressed willingness to discuss maintaining relations with the French Union and protecting French commercial and cultural interests in Vietnam. This was a position far stronger than Britain was willing to accept.

The Soviet negotiating position, revealed a few days later, was more flexible and represented a considerable drawing away from Pham Van Dong's demand for a unified and independent Vietnam. The Soviet position, which became the framework that the conference accepted and worked from, proposed discussing five questions: 1. a cease-fire; 2. the creation of zones for the regroupment of forces; 3. means to prevent military buildups after the cease-fire; 4. a supervisory body to control the arrangements; 5. guarantees of implementation. Pham Van Dong finally accepted this framework, withdrawing his proposals.

The Chinese, too, with Russian agreement, were responsible for modifying the Vietminh demands. For instance, Pham Van Dong at one point retreated from his position on Pathet Lao and Khmer national rights to the creation of an autonomous Pathet Lao government in two Laotian provinces. Chou En-lai, after conferring with Mendes-France, withdrew support for even this more moderate Vietminh demand. Lancaster said: "Chou En-Lai's 'betrayal' is reported to have reduced [Pham Van] Dong to a state of suppressed fury and to have clouded subsequent relations between the Vietminh and Chinese delegations."[6]

The Soviet plan regarding Europe worked. Molotov gave an unusually bitter speech against Bidault during the middle of the conference, arousing feeling in the French National Assembly that the existing French leadership was standing in the way of a negotiated settlement. On June 12 a vote of no confidence brought down Laniel and Bidault; a new Government was formed on June 17. Its head, Mendes-France, pledged an honorable settlement by July 20. The settlement was achieved only a few hours after the deadline, and the parties left Geneva with the Communist delegations declaring the conference a success. Shortly thereafter, true to the bar-

[6] *The Emancipation of French Indochina*, p. 334.

gain, Mendes-France campaigned against the EDC on the grounds that it would not accept certain of his proposed "qualifications," including, for example, veto rights for the member countries and an eight-year postponement of the provisions calling for a supranational force. His amendments turned down by the other EDC members, he returned to open the long-awaited National Assembly debate on joining the EDC. In August, said Lancaster, the proposal was "implicitly and ignominiously rejected on a mere question of procedure."[7]

There was an obvious way, however, in which the Geneva Conference was not a success. Soviet diplomacy could not prevent the U.S. and the Saigon Government from refusing to accept the terms of settlement and, instead, inaugurating a new Government in South Vietnam in violation of the Agreements. The U.S. puppet Diem could barely form a Government. Lancaster reported that he would have been overthrown by his Army had it not been for American announcements that aid would be channeled only to Diem. Once in power, Diem stated, as the present rulers in Saigon still state today, that no negotiations with Hanoi were possible. According to Geneva, there were to be consultations between the two Governments in 1955 followed by a general election in 1956. When it was clear that the agreements were not going to be respected, Pham Van Dong and others appealed again and again for pressure from the Geneva Powers, including the Soviet Union, Britain, and the International Control Commission. Nothing was forthcoming besides statements. As Lancaster summarized:

Although Dong approached Molotov again in November [1955] with a request that measures should be concerted with the British Government to ensure that the Geneva Agreements

---

[7] *Ibid.,* pp. 336–337.

were respected, his plea proved ineffectual as the Soviet Government, whose policy was now directed to easing international tensions, was reluctant to resort to coercive measures.[8]

Philippe Devillers, a Frenchman who lived in Indochina during the war years, and whose histories of Vietnam are standard works, described this period as "the occasion for the great powers to bury the Vietnamese problem."[9] It was on France that the Vietnamese counted, he said, quoting Pham Van Dong's January 1, 1955, appeal to the French. The Vietnamese thought the French would support them because, first, France was the only Great Power that had both signed the accords and had troops in Vietnam; second, the French "democratic" leadership would support the cause of nationalism in Vietnam; third, "France, disappointed or exasperated by the affronts offered them by the followers of Diem, might change partners and gamble on unification (in agreement with the North) in order to maintain her presence in Vietnam."

But the desire for disengagement in Indochina, which had been fostered among the French people, was too strong to permit new tensions to develop over the implementation of the Geneva Agreements. Especially was this the case with the new war in Algeria building up. Thus France pulled out of Vietnam, in accord with the letter of the Agreements, but the consequence was that there were no French forces—no means—to implement the Agreements regarding reunification.

When the Vietnamese protested, Devillers said, they learned a lesson about the "importance which the great powers attached to the problems of their small allies."[10] The Great Powers became involved primarily because they feared a

[8] *Ibid.*, p. 372.
[9] *Vietnam*, ed. Gettleman, p. 219.
[10] *Ibid.*, p. 218.

renewal of war along the 17th parallel. The Chinese suggested a new Geneva Conference. The Soviet Union and Great Britain proposed that the International Control Commission, supposed to be a temporary body with no enforcement powers, maintain its offices if necessary beyond the 1956 date of the proposed election. As for the election, which Saigon announced its refusal to enter, the Russians and British "merely enjoined" the two Vietnamese Governments to make an announcement whenever they arrived at an agreement to consult or hold elections. Between 1956 and 1960, Hanoi over and over appealed to Saigon to begin consultations about the election. Each time their messages were met "with scornful silences or stinging replies." In addition, on each occasion "Soviet and Chinese support was restricted to kind words, warm gestures of solidarity, and propaganda campaigns."[11] In 1957, the year after reunification was to occur, the Soviet Union proposed at the United Nations the simultaneous admission of the two Vietnams, thus giving legitimacy to the idea of a permanent division despite the conclusions of the conference which the Soviets had chaired three years earlier. And, as in the past, Hanoi was persuaded to accept Soviet judgment, in part perhaps because North Vietnam was dependent on the Russians for precious food shipments since the division of the country had cut the North off from the rich rice and fish of the South. Hanoi took the position that a long struggle was commencing, and that socialism should be built in the North as a prerequisite to supporting the movement for reunification. The North Vietnamese maintained the view that their Southern brothers should still use nonviolent means of struggle. Hanoi began a propaganda campaign against the American

11 *Ibid.*, p. 219.

violation of Geneva, in hopes of winning world public opinion in its behalf.[12]

But in the South, the former Vietminh partisans could not abide by the policy of nonviolent struggle permanently in the face of Diem's campaign to wipe them out. Bernard Fall

[12] One of the points on which we differ from our traveling companion Herbert Aptheker is that we believe, as the foregoing treatment of the Geneva Conference indicates, that Vietnamese revolutionaries have not only been betrayed by the Western Great Powers but have received much less than full support from the Communist Great Powers, in particular the Soviet Union.

The matter is of such importance to our entire approach in this book that we should like to quote from three other treatments of Geneva, each by researchers connected with the independent anti-war movement in the United States:

1. John McDermott, *A Profile of Vietnamese History* (New York, 1965), p. 8: ". . . the Russians were interested in using concessions in the Far East to obtain European objectives. . . . Soviet diplomacy was willing to make substantial concessions to the French on the Vietnamese question in return for French cooperation in blocking the EDC. In fact, EDC failed in September 1954 for lack of French support; there is good evidence that the French were repaying their debts from Geneva. . . . China followed the lead of her wealthier socialist neighbor, and worked to achieve a cease-fire."

2. American Friends Service Committee, *Peace in Vietnam* (New York, 1966), p. 41: "The Vietminh was reluctant to agree to this partition [along the 17th parallel], which left it with slightly less than half of the territory of Vietnam, despite the fact that at the time it controlled three-quarters. However, Ho Chi Minh's government was under strong Soviet and Chinese pressure to give way on this point. The concern of China, and probably also the Soviet Union, was that continuation of the war might cause the introduction of American military power—possibly atomic—in support of the French, a course of action which the United States did in fact come very close to taking."

3. Adam Schesch and Frances Prevas, *An Outline History of Viet-Nam* (Madison, 1965; prepared for the University of Wisconsin Student-Faculty Committee to End the War in Vietnam), pp. 11–12: "The United States kept up the threat of full-scale military intervention in Indochina in order to get the Vietminh to accept . . . an unfavorable settlement at Geneva. The Russians on the other hand were also applying pressure on the Vietminh. Concerned with their position in Europe, with the possibility of the European Defense Community, they were willing to sacrifice the interests of the nationalist movement and of the Vietnamese Communist Party within that movement. . . .

pointed out that they maintained a "prudently calm attitude" from 1954 to 1956.[13] Thereafter, however, the Resistance broke out in place after place.

Faced with this situation, what could Hanoi do? Devillers asked: could it "stick to this policy of 'peaceful co-existence' when its result was, in effect, to allow the Diem police to proceed with impunity to take their toll of the best elements in the Party?" He replied that the result was an alteration of Hanoi policy reflected in the 1960 Party debate. That was the year of the major Soviet-Albanian fight, and it was carried over into the question of Vietnam. At the Vietnamese Party convention in September, the key questions were those related to support for the Southern struggle. "We have every reason to think that Moscow counselled prudence," said Devillers.[14] On the ideological plane, the more moderate Soviet statements were accepted. But the Party acknowledged that the process of active support for the South had to begin. Some aid already had been given early in the year, and now Ho Chi Minh argued that "greater efforts" should be made at reunification, and a former South Vietnamese partisan, Le Duan, was elected

---

"The nationalist movement in Vietnam, though victorious on the battle field was subject to great pressures from both the Western and Eastern powers to make concessions to the French. Seeking national unity, the Vietminh asked for national elections to be held within a year. The French insisted on a two year period. The French also got the Vietminh to give up a large part of the territory they held: the truce line was moved back from the thirteenth parallel where the Vietminh was firmly in control, to the seventeenth. . . .

"The threat of massive American intervention and pressure for a settlement from Russia and China forced the Vietminh to agree to the partition of their country."

[13] Fall, "Viet-Cong—The Unseen Enemy in Viet-Nam," *Viet-Nam Reader*, ed. Raskin and Fall, p. 254.

[14] Devillers, *Vietnam*, ed. Gettleman, p. 228.

Party general secretary. This was the beginning of the change which still continues.[15]

IV

This tale of Soviet diplomatic caution toward the struggle in Vietnam seemed the more believable after talking with members of the Soviet Peace Committee in Moscow at Christmastime, and again at Geneva in June.

Here are some Soviet attitudes which were expressed to us.

We dined with the foreign policy editor of a Moscow newspaper. As Soviet couples circled the floor to jazz which would be typical, if dated, in the United States, Staughton raised the question, whether if social revolutions spread in the underdeveloped nations, the United States would feel cornered and strike out desperately against the socialist world. To our astonishment, our Russian friend threw up his hands and said: "Capitalism, socialism, what is the difference? There only are poor countries and rich countries. If your businessmen were not so stupid, together we could build up the poorer countries like India."

A woman who interpreted for us, and has hosted a number

[15] Precisely the same Soviet attitude is reported in the same period toward the Algerian revolution. Adolfo Gilly said: "The Algerian people have not forgotten that the French Communist Party, at the beginning of the armed revolution in Algeria, denounced it as a 'nationalist and reactionary' movement. . . . Neither have the people forgotten that the Algerian Communist Party followed the line of the French Communist Party [nor] the diplomatic considerations that kept Khrushchev from giving arms to Algeria and made him appear instead to be friendly with a French government in open imperialist warfare against the Algerian people." (Preface, Frantz Fanon, *Studies in a Dying Colonialism* [New York, 1965], p. 10).

of important American visitors, asked us in Moscow on our return from Peking: "Do the Chinese still dress alike? Do they ever smile?" Later in Geneva, she told Staughton: "We were just like the Chinese after our Revolution, but you'll see, when life is easier for them, they will think differently." She seemed to feel it was unfair for a small nation of thirty million people to create a danger of nuclear war for two hundred million Russians and for the whole world.

Finally, we spoke both in Moscow and Geneva with a distinguished Soviet historian and member of the Soviet Peace Committee Presidium, whose view was that the "transition from capitalism to socialism" was a complex process which might take centuries and which did not necessarily entail world wars or violent revolutions.

But that was only half the story. The lady interpreter said bitterly that she would not visit the United States until the war in Vietnam ended. And at a meeting with the full Presidium of the Peace Committee, when Staughton began to describe how difficult it was for Americans to argue for peace while the other side refuses to negotiate, the chairman became angry and attacked Staughton for insensitivity to American aggression.

Thus we think the Chinese view of Soviet behavior toward Vietnam has historical justification but is exaggerated. The exaggeration lies in the assumption that Soviet complicity in the maintenance of American power is conscious and deliberate. We think that complicity developed pragmatically, and may very well not continue if American policy moves in the direction of more Vietnams. Just as in 1954 the Russians traded a compromise peace in Vietnam for French withdrawal from EDC, so today they may soften their support of the N.L.F. in order to keep Germany from getting nuclear arms. Our impression, however, is that much as the Soviets may desire to reach an accommodation with the United States on European problems, they will hesitate to do so as long as there is war in Vietnam.

Further, while we can understand the Chinese contention that revolutionaries must not be deterred by threats from the United States of nuclear "massive retaliation," still we think the Russians are right in insisting on the qualitatively different nature of nuclear war. The possibility of nuclear violence presents to the aspiring revolutionary a fundamental dilemma. If he persists in his efforts he may unleash the nuclear holocaust. Because those who have made their revolutions are now led by fear to discourage others from doing likewise is no reason to maintain that the dilemma does not exist.

If the Chinese exaggerate Russian conservatism, it is minuscule compared to America's exaggeration of Chinese aggressiveness. The same American analysts who urged President Kennedy to seek détente with the Soviet Union now urge that the containment once practiced against Russia in Europe should now be practiced against China in Asia. Thus George F. Kennan told the Senate Committee on Foreign Relations at its 1966 hearings on China that Mao and his colleagues exhibit "an extremely difficult and almost hysterical state of mind . . . highly excitable and irritated." Kennan continued: "I think there is little opportunity of talking with them or dealing effectively with them today." While somewhat more enlightened than Representative Lyndon Johnson's reference to "yellow dwarfs" in 1948, Ivy League analysis and Texas prejudice lead to the same conclusion. Perhaps—the argument goes—when the present leadership departs from the Chinese stage and revolutionary China prospers and mellows as has the Soviet Union, America can cooperate with China. But for the moment, although it may be possible to render China less "isolated" (particularly when one is about to lose in the United Nations anyway), China must be "contained" by firm resistance to its foreign adventures as in Vietnam.

To this apparent consensus among American liberal scholars, we fundamentally object on three counts.

First, the analogy so cherished by American policy-makers between Nazi aggression in the nineteen-thirties and Communist expansion today, is not valid in Asia. It had a limited validity in Europe, especially in the spring of 1945. At that time the Russian Army, no doubt, wished to move as far West as possible, leaving in its wake governments whose foreign policy would not be hostile to the Soviet Union. But even then the Russians were not prepared to risk war for the sake of, say, Communism in France or Italy. From 1947 to 1962 the analogy was kept alive by forebodings about a Russian sweep to the English channel. As many American generals said at the time, that threat was always a paper bear. The Russians had no such intention and the Americans knew it. But events in Berlin, Czechoslovakia, and Korea sufficiently confirmed the stereotype of Russian military aggression that the analogy to the nineteen-thirties retained its hold on the American mind.

In Asia, however, there is general agreement that Communist-led revolutions of discontented peasants rather than outright military aggression constitute the primary Communist threat to American interests. Even were the U.S. State Department right in viewing the N.L.F. as "aggression from the North," it still would be a Vietnamese, not a Chinese, North. Those who have sought to reorient discussion of the Vietnam war to China, as the alleged basic problem in the area, wrongly accept the American Government's assumption that China is behind it all. They help America to present itself not as a bully practicing near-genocide against a nation one-sixth its size, but as a valiant underdog holding the line against seven hundred and fifty million Chinese. They distract attention from the real problem for American foreign policy, which is not response to China but response to the revolutionary Third World.

Second, we think that Chinese Communism may depart from the "laws of development" suggested by the Russian model. Certainly it will if the Chinese themselves have any influence on events. Preventing a recurrence in their own society of the tendency toward bureaucracy, parochial nationalism, and corruption which they see in their Russian neighbor seemed to concern the Chinese more than any other issue, including American imperialism. Tang Ming-chao put it this way: "Marx never said stop being a revolutionary when you gain power. We must be revolutionary. We must be one with the people of the world. We must prevent the emergence of a privileged group here. You see, there is a class struggle in socialist society. It is not in the sense of working class against the bourgeoisie but it is non-antagonistic, a set of conflicts among the people which can only be solved by democracy." The Chinese determination, that human will and clear ideology shall prevail and prevent the operation of tendencies toward decay, is evident in their summary of the four key attitudes for a revolutionary. The "four firsts" are: 1. human factors are more important than material factors; 2. political work is the most important kind of work; 3. ideas are first; 4. living ideas take precedence over old ideas. "The relations of production are very important," Tang commented, "but the superstructure—the relations of individuals—is very important too."

We think America may make a serious mistake if it assumes that these are the ideas only of an older generation which experienced the Revolution personally. Every resource of the largest society on earth is being harnessed so that they will prevail among the youth, as well.

The third and most serious fallacy in transferring to Asia the Nazi analogy and the containment strategy is that America not China has been the fundamental aggressor in their relationship.

Tang Ming-chao traced the development of Chinese attitudes toward America since World War II for us. He said: "We knew the history of the United States in China. But during World War II America's actions were partly good and partly bad. We couldn't decide if they would become worse." (Staughton can recall that in 1946-48 it was the Chinese who argued in the world Communist movement that a third world war was not inevitable, just as in the early nineteen-fifties it was the Chinese who first advanced "coexistence" as a policy toward India.)

"One year with [George C.] Marshall, however, made us conclude that the United States would be against us. Korea deepened the conviction. That war was really aimed at China, as is the Vietnam war."

Tang then described the ambassadorial contacts at Warsaw which followed the Geneva Agreements. "We proposed an unrestricted exchange of journalists, and the release of United States prisoners from the Korean War if Chinese students in the United States were permitted to return to the mainland. What happened? The agreement on exchange of journalists had apparently been completed when Secretary Dulles intervened and said he would have to approve personally each American who went. We released all but four POW's, but the United States did not release any Chinese students. We would also have been interested in the exchange of students."

(When we returned to the United States, Staughton had the opportunity to ask Harrison E. Salisbury of the *New York Times* if this version of post-Geneva transactions between the U.S. and China was correct. Salisbury replied that it was a little condensed but substantially true. So much for the President's statement that China "always hangs up the phone.")

Tang's comments about current outstanding issues between the two countries again suggested complexity and restraint. He said: "Hong Kong? Khrushchev used to urge us to take it. But that would make a very serious crisis which the people of the world would not understand. The United States would use it politically and militarily. We believe in the opposite of pre-emptive war.

"Taiwan, in contrast, is an internal affair. The United States should withdraw its fleet. It is our business whether we use force. If the Seventh Fleet withdraws, we will have a third united front with Chiang Kai-shek.

"The admission of China to the United Nations without a change in the status of Taiwan is impossible. We are grateful to those who try to secure our admission, but the United States must change its policy of hostility first. Would the United Nations be viable in the future? We'll see.

"I wouldn't worry a bit about India. It is not essential. We are not going to fight them. They had a taste in 1962. We have to look at the people of the world. The reactionaries have spread so much propaganda against us. India has been oppressed so long they don't like anyone to conquer their country."

This then was the voice of today's Red Menace. It was a sophisticated voice, never, so far as we could tell, a wantonly cruel voice, albeit an utterly hard and determined voice. Perhaps the United States would do well to apply to its own rhetoric about China the standard we so often apply to the propaganda of the other side: deeds, not words. When the Seventh Fleet leaves the Taiwan Strait, America can begin to talk convincingly about Chinese aggression. When China kills its first Vietnamese and the United States its last, we will know that it is they, rather than we, who are anxious to "fight to the last Vietnamese."

9

REVOLUTION
AND VIOLENCE I:
AS THEY SEE IT

I

How should we think about these Vietnamese who turn to violence and revolution? As we interviewed our "enemies," we groped to understand what kind of experience, what kind of values visiting foreigners like ourselves could use to judge men whose lives were so different from our own.

One of our conclusions was to let the Vietnamese, through our interviews, tell in their own words why they adopted the methods they did in pursuit of justice. Those we met in Prague, Moscow, and Peking were eloquent in defense of their Government and revolution, but their authoritativeness was weakened somewhat by their distance as diplomats from the continuing experience in Vietnam. In Hanoi, we finally encountered some actual fighters from the South: heroes of the N.L.F. Army who were traveling and speaking in North Vietnam. We also met a delegate to the North Vietnamese

Assembly who was from the South and spoke of conditions there with special knowledge and intensity.

The setting, as we finally came face-to-face with enemy soldiers, was a hotel lobby with TV cameras and the inevitable tea. The heroes were dressed in light green uniforms (this since has led us to wonder about identification of enemy soldiers in the South as "North Vietnamese regulars" because they wear khaki uniforms). Heavily decorated, they were incredibly small and youthful in appearance. Their leader, Huynh Van Danh, presented to us as the veteran of more than one hundred battles, must have been less than five feet tall.

Clearly they had told their stories many times and clearly, too, they knew that their function was to be inspirational. Oanh, our interpreter, told us afterward that our questions presumed too much sophistication. It was plain to us that Oanh profoundly admired them, but nevertheless regarded them primarily as activists. For whatever reason, the heroes did tend to speak to us in generalities. The few nuggets of biographical information and personal comment that we extracted seemed the more precious. All that we quote of their remarks was said with an intensity which we could only compare to that of SNCC workers discussing civil rights in the United States.

Huynh Van Danh, from Tan Tru district in Long An province, spoke of the Diem Government's repression. "For example, in my village they forced people to sleep collectively in a common house. They tortured those whose families had gone to the North," he said. The purpose of the war against the French was independence but afterward there was no independence. "What alternative did we have than to stand up? We realize that American people, especially young people, don't want to fight in Vietnam."

There was one girl in the group of five, Ta Thi Kieu from Ben Tre province. She was twenty-six years old and had been in thirty-three battles. She too began by speaking of the Diem regime. People had been tortured and disemboweled; women had been raped; young men were press-ganged for the Army. "Comparing South Vietnam with Hitler, the crimes in the former seem to me greater." Kieu made a significant statement: "In my village land had been distributed during the Resistance." At first, she said, the struggle against Diem had been political. There were protests against jailings, against the press-gang. "But the more we carried out political struggle the more terrorism and suppression increased." So armed struggle began, at first with bamboo sticks, booby traps, no rifles. The villagers divided the land again, helped each other with production.

"If you were in our position," Kieu said simply, "you would have no other way than what we are doing."

Later she stressed again the construction of a new society in the midst of war. "In the liberated areas there are no very rich or very poor," Kieu asserted. "There is bombing and strafing but life is developing. It's not true that North Vietnam is invading. The whole Vietnamese people want to live together as one family."

The same emphasis was repeated by Tran Duong (pronounced "Zuong") from Quang Nam province. His mother had been killed by the French, his father by Diem. In the liberated areas, he said, there is enough food and clothing. "The children can go to school and study."

Vai, a member of a minority group, did not speak at all. The oldest of the heroes was twenty-nine-year-old Le Chi Nguyen. He is an explosives expert and, in contrast to all the others, a member of the N.L.F. regular Army as distinct from its local and guerrilla contingents.

We had asked about how the war of the Front began and mentioned the allegation in the United States that Vietminh cadres had buried their arms in violation of the Geneva Agreements. "Although I was young," observed Nguyen, "I saw the people's armed forces regroup to the North." Some arms had been dug up by the Diem regime which the French had left behind for their henchmen, he said.

Was it true that the Front forced young men to join its Army? Nguyen denied this, too: "The Front never forces young people to join the Army. It is the puppet Army which does this. We young people never submitted to the enemy. We didn't want to be slaves. That is why we stood up with sticks or stones in our hands. Joining the Army is the aspiration of the people." Nguyen went on to express in his own way the sentiment most frequently repeated to us in Vietnam. "We distinguish between the American Government and the people," he began in the familiar vein. "At present the United States Government is trying to press-gang young Americans for the Army. That's why there appears the example of Norman Morrison. As a laboring person, I love American laboring people. But I hate American aggressors."

As we rose to go Nguyen took Staughton's hand in a grip of steel, looked him in the eyes, and said, "Please tell the American people that we do not want to kill American soldiers. But"—this was the second most common phrase we heard— "there can be no real peace until we are independent."

The meeting with the guerrillas was too brief and too hurried for our purposes, as each person spoke only once or twice, but our hosts explained the heroes were visiting relatives of Southerners. Perhaps our best opportunity to understand the thinking of the Vietnamese revolutionary came in our talk with Nguyen Minh Vy, identified to us as an "expert on the situation in the South."

We met Vy, a member of the North Vietnam Peace Committee, in the small hotel dining room. His South Vietnamese home is near Camranh Bay, where the United States is building a military base described by James Reston in 1965 as "being constructed on a scale far larger than is necessary to care for the present level of American forces."[1]

A man of perhaps forty-five years, with a fresh and good-natured attitude, he carried no notes, and his face reflected eagerness to speak with us "from the heart" about his subject. As his words and feelings filled those plain surroundings for three hours, we felt, as did our interpreter Oanh, engaged more in a drama than an interview. He began with the proud sentiment we had heard before: "Vietnam is one country. We had our national power earlier than the western countries."

We quote as exactly as we can his explanation of why the Vietnamese are taking up arms.

"For us, independence means the chance for existence, since two million people starved in the nineteen-forties. This is still very strong, very close and recent—it is the truth itself.

"Even during the Resistance not all the territory of South Vietnam was occupied by the French. There were many large free areas. The policy of 'people's democratic power' was carried out, especially the right of the peasants to the land. The administration of the Resistance did this."

Staughton, who as an historian is interested in the movement of tenant farmers during the American Revolution, especially appreciated Vy's comparison of American and Vietnamese experience: "What is recent history here is old history to the American people. Peasants requesting their land is something very remote to your people.

"You don't understand how wretched the peasants were. When the Resistance solved the problem of the land, there was happiness and great uprising in the countryside. The concrete

[1] *New York Times*, August 27, 1965.

meaning of independence was to safeguard your land. That is why Ho has great prestige, because the Resistance did this for the peasants in the South.

"In the cities, too, a Resistance administration developed. The present public health officer of the D.R.V. was Resistance administrator in Saigon.

"He who can resist foreign aggression can have prestige among the people, and prestige will be greater if he wins."

On the way to Hanoi, many Vietnamese had told us that the 1954 Geneva provision which "regrouped" the armed forces of both sides into the two temporary zones, North and South, was extremely painful since it split apart families and separated men from their home provinces. Ho's Resistance Army and Administration went North; left behind was all the territory—half of South Vietnam—which had been cleared of French control. We asked Vy, himself a Southerner, to describe some of the effects of this regroupment.

"Those who lived in the free areas were forced to accept a hostile Administration. It is not an easy thing for those who have been free to have their land taken back. Those of us who had to regroup to the North were never glad with that. In those days Ho himself was obliged to issue a special appeal to people of South Vietnam to carry out the Geneva Agreement[s]. He appealed—only to him would the South Vietnamese listen. He said, Southern compatriots have to sacrifice their immediate interest for long-term interests of peace and independence.

"When the Diem regime was formed, the people of South Vietnam knew very well what would happen because Diem was an agent of the French before. He committed many crimes against his compatriots under the label of exterminating Communists. The French used to call every patriot Communist. This is because it creates confusion for the people. But it is also very good because it makes people see that the greatest patriots are Communists.

"The U.S. aided the French before. It was very clear to people what would happen. People do not need theory, only some experience. How did the South Vietnamese people think when they had to accept hostility, when the Resistance moved back to the North? First, they were very anxious. They knew beforehand that Diem would bring back what was done by the French before. The U.S. was more clever than the French in the first years, using indirect means of influence, neo-colonialism. They took away the independence we had gained against Japan and the French. . . .

"Reality helps people understand better. Diem was terrible. Kennedy himself had to do away with Diem,[2] but in a 1960 election speech he had made a eulogy to Diem. What did Diem do? He was a feudal official. He defended the rights of the

[2] *The Politics of Escalation* has this to say concerning United States responsibility for Diem's fall (p. 24):

During the summer prior to the coup, there had been three and a half months of Buddhist street demonstrations. Retrospectively, it has been suggested that it was these demonstrations and American sympathy for them that led to the coup. News reports of the time tell a different story. The Buddhist demonstrations had effectively been cut off on August 21, 1963, by the repressive raid of Vietnamese Special Forces (in U.S. pay). Thus it was not the demonstrations that triggered the coup; rather, the moving cause seems to have been the announcement by the U.S. Embassy in Saigon on October 21 that United States pay for the South Vietnamese Special Forces would be terminated unless these Forces were employed in the field against the Communists. (*New York Times*, October 22, 1963). Under this U.S. pressure, Diem and Nhu were reluctantly compelled to send their Special Forces out of the capital on October 30; left without their elite guard, the brothers fell within hours.

Journalist David Halberstam reported that Ambassador Lodge visited Diem the morning of the coup with knowledge that it would occur but said nothing to the South Vietnamese President. (*New York Times*, November 6, 1963).

landlords, of the comprador capitalists [Vietnamese managers representing the French]; he opposed the Resistance. This is why when he was in power it was logical for him to recover the peasant land and give it back to the landlords. He carried out reprisals too against former members of the Resistance."[3]

To the State Department charge that Ho's Vietminh secretly left men behind in the South to carry on subversion, Vy had this to say. "According to Geneva, just troops had to regroup. This means those with arms in hand had to regroup to the North. But it doesn't mean all Resistance members. Otherwise, the whole population would have drawn to the North, for nearly everybody participated in the people's Resistance against the French.

"There is a very just provision in the Geneva Agreements: that there be no reprisals and discrimination against those who cooperated with the opposite side. The same with the North. When French troops withdrew, very many of the people who cooperated with them stayed, such as people at the Polytechnic Institute.

"My own family knew there would be reprisals. But to insure peace we obeyed Ho. Because there was an international

[3] Article 14, Section C of the Agreement on Cessation of Hostilities states: "Each party undertakes to refrain from any reprisals or discrimination against persons or organizations on account of their activities during the hostilities and to guarantee their democratic liberties." The February, 1955, interim report of the International Control Commission concluded that there was "room for improvement in the implementation by both parties of the Articles of the Agreement dealing with democratic freedoms"; but the sixth interim ICC report supports Vy's charges: ". . . the degree of co-operation given to the Commission by the two parties has not been the same. While the Commission has experienced difficulties in North Vietnam, the major part of its difficulties has arisen in South Vietnam." (*Vietnam*, ed. Gettleman, pp. 140–141, 166–167, 172).

Bernard Fall has estimated that eighty thousand Vietminh went North of the 17th parallel while perhaps five thousand remained in the South.

agreement we thought there were possibilities of implementing it.

"We didn't believe the Americans would carry out these agreements. That Mr. Bedell Smith, representing the United States, did not sign them was already a warning. South Vietnam didn't sign. It was right for them not to sign because they were defeated." He laughed. "This made us better understand our enemy.

"But what is the basic problem? For us, the Vietnamese people, the greatest problem was the provision to carry out the unification of the country, to hold general elections in 1956 under supervision. If this had happened, I would have been back in South Vietnam in 1956."

Here he fell into half-humorous, half-sentimental reflections on the South. "There are not very big differences between South and North, although there we have no winters like these. Whenever winter comes, I want to go back South. I must tell you this. Every year when winter comes there is this same feeling among thousands of people here in the North.

"Suppose Diem had carried out the Geneva Agreement[s]. The situation would be different. But it was terrible, worse under Diem than in thousands of years. For example, I carried out anti-French activities and was arrested. The French arrested for concrete crimes, for example, the flagrant distribution of leaflets. But Diem imprisoned people ideologically. They were arrested without evidence. The police said: 'You are a former Resistance member, therefore you are Communist.' They told you to tear down the photo of Ho and the Red Flag to be set free. Otherwise, they said you would be imprisoned forever. In the six years, 1954–59, one hundred and fifty thousand were killed. Another example is Poulo Condor Island where the French used to imprison exiles. This is hell.

Under the French, for example, women would not be detained in this prison. But Diem put men and women there together. People were arrested for intentions, not deeds.

"Regarding the wives of those regrouped to the North, I am unclear. But the majority have their families remaining in South Vietnam. A cruel Diem policy was to force those wives to declare a divorce in public, to abandon their husbands. If they did not want to abandon them, the police said it meant they still loved their husbands and therefore they have a sympathy for the Communists."[4]

As he spoke about the "pacification" program of the U.S.–backed regime, we understood more clearly how the paternal attitude of the Saigon Government led to a completely unrealistic program of rural reform. The 1966 "Honolulu Agreement" was not new, but the latest in a series of plans going back over the years. The pattern is to break up village life, group the people into large hamlets surrounded by barbed wire and heavily guarded, then burn the jungle and fields around the hamlets to isolate the N.L.F. Army. Vy explained the reasons for the peasants' rejection of this "aid" from Saigon.[5]

---

[4] Denis Warner told of the separation of families:

All over the South before the Viet Minh evacuation late in 1954, hundreds, even thousands, of weddings took place. At the worst, it seemed, the separation would be for two years. In Quang Ngai, one of the poorest of all provinces in Central Vietnam, but also one with great strategic importance, more than 500 of these weddings were celebrated, and some 20,000 families there have close relatives in the North. (*The Last Confucian*, p. 142).

[5] Western sources corroborate Vy's analysis of the strategic hamlets. Homer Bigart reported that in one area only seventy families would "volunteer" to go into the hamlets while one hundred and thirty-five families were "herded forcibly" by troops. (*New York Times*, March 29, 1962). Four years later, a fifth pacification effort is underway but it "differs largely in name from its predecessors." (*New York Times*,

"For an industrially developed country it is very easy for people to live concentrated. Even in parts of North Vietnam the villagers are rather concentrated. The villagers live within the borders of a bamboo fence. Specific relationships develop among people. The people in South Vietnam, however, live very sparsely, especially the people in the mountains. They still are very backward. They live completely free. They feel the absolute significance of freedom. They want no one to sow any trouble. They have their own guns, their own land, their own fish ponds—each individual is a separate economy. They eat the rice they produce, eat the fish from the brooks. They fabricate their own clothes. What are they, if they are concentrated into one place, put in narrow houses! They must get permission to till the land. They go out in the morning and come back in the evening just like buffaloes and oxen. Forced labor, heavy taxes, children forced into the Army—if they oppose this, they are considered Communists. They cannot bear it. It is impossible to live. This is the reason for the fall of Diem. Diem had learned these programs from the British in Malaysia; also the French did it here with their 'agrovilles.' When people's houses are burned down, they have to find another resting place. You in the West wouldn't know what a house means to the Vietnamese peasant. A house was built three generations ago because people were very poor: sort of property to be given heirs for generations.

"Psychologically speaking, there are two things which most

October 20, 1966). The South Vietnamese director of the program himself said pacification has led to "old life" rather than "new life" hamlets which the Government orders the people to build. The *Times* report added that the "difficulty in all the programs has not been the planning, most of which has been sound, but the implementation."

people hate. One is to dig up the graves of ancestors and the other is to burn down houses. Diem committed both those things. Also he cut down fruit trees: for example, orange trees grown for many generations to bear fruit. When people refused to go into strategic hamlets there was massive killing. Following the tradition of the imperialists, the Diemists said, 'Kill to make an example.'

"It was unbearable. There was only one alternative for South Vietnam. There was no hope for Diem to carry out the Geneva accords. Three years after Geneva there had not been elections. Life became harder. If you asked to live in your former house, you were considered Communist and you were killed. Well, there was no other way."

Out of these conditions grew the new civil war in the Southern zone.

"The movement of struggle gained momentum after 1959. Until that time the people only urged Diem to carry out the Geneva accords, demanded insurance of freedom and rights, demanded their land. It was not sufficient to demand all those things. The main thing to demand was to live. Diem didn't give hope of living. Therefore the people had to defend themselves with arms in hand. This, I think, everyone knows, because the American Government itself said the lack of success was the fault of Diem."

II

Tom asked if someone less brutal than Diem would have won the people. "Many people said, If there is another one better than Diem, that would be better for the U.S. But he himself was the best for the Americans. No one was available after Diem. Besides for our people, the greatest problem is foreign aggression. The anti-aggression feeling is deep into our blood. This is why anyone who acts as an agent for foreign aggression can never stand. Our people are very sensible on this. Ky was a pilot for the French from 1950 to 1953. Most people in Saigon today were working for the French Army. Diem was just the cleverest pleader for the imperialists.

"In eighty years with the French, two million people starved. Only five years under Diem, one hundred and fifty thousand were killed and one million were arrested and imprisoned. This is why the people had to rise in opposition.

"It is the U.S. Government that has created Diem and equipped his Administration to fight our people. They used Diem to create a sort of position for the United States in South Vietnam. When it was considered to be necessary to replace Diem, the same types came in. Ky says his hero is Hitler.

"Understand the state of mind of the South Vietnamese people, how the people of the whole country think of South Vietnam. Well, Vietnam is one, not two different peoples. People in the South never opposed the people in the North. The United States used to say that Southerners opposed the North. This is not the same as in, say, Sudan. Also, because of regroupment, there are South Vietnamese in the North. Their feelings are separated. Frankly speaking, we from South Vietnam cannot stand it when we look at a map. This is the same feeling everyone has; it is very profoundly a feeling of unity. This does not mean North Vietnamese encroachment, because not only history but even the Geneva Agreements recognize the unity of our country. It is not a problem of two nations, as Dean Rusk used to say. Our people's sentiment is very unified."

At this point, Oanh, our interpreter, was crying.

"Now our compatriots in the South have arisen in political and military struggle against American troops. The question is how they are waging the war. Just one point, if I'm able to say it, because I am a Southerner myself. You see, we used to say South Vietnam can only fight with the assistance of the North. But there are fourteen million South Vietnamese. Cuba has only six million people. When the people can stand it no longer, no matter how few they are, they will be able to do something. The people of South Vietnam very eagerly desire independence because they already had independence during the Resistance. The peasants had land; they cannot stand it when it is taken.

"We used to talk to each other like this . . . a hungry man, when he never tasted a biscuit, he doesn't know, but once he has eaten it, he knows it is delicious. Now if he loses it, he really lost something. Or if he is given a false biscuit, the more he desires the former biscuit he had.

"Then there's another thing that such people get when they struggle for thousands of years. They are very rich in experience, and they can do anything themselves. Anyone can practice guerrilla warfare. Some of them can occupy enemy strongposts bare-handed.

"They are waging a very clever political struggle too: demanding democratic liberties, forcing the Saigon Administration to try to solve their requests, not to have killings, not to have villages bombed. My own experience is too obsolete to tell you further. But anyone there can wage political and guerrilla struggles: they are forced to out of experience. At the beginning their weapons were very primitive. It's not only me saying this, but the American press says it. They were shooting with powder and nails and bolts from bicycles, with a sort of handmade detonator. They wait for the enemy to come within a distance of ten meters before firing. From such primitive conditions, they took over modern weapons from the enemy. I don't know why Western oppressors can't understand. We do it very clearly. During the French aggression in the South, we tried by every means to equip ourselves with captured weapons.

"It's clear that the American troops cannot cope with the situation. What is the reason? The rapid growth of the N.L.F. The West says this is because of terrorism. The greater terrorist is Diem. If to say you can win people by acts of terror, then Diem must succeed in winning the people! This is a question of truth which I think some in the West either cannot understand or they are obstinate in trying to understand."

Staughton asked Vy's opinion of the charge that the N.L.F. kills technicians and civil servants. He replied: "I cannot replace the N.L.F. to give an answer, but I would like to ask, what for? If the N.L.F. carries out those deeds, what for? No reason. First, this is fabrication and why is because the N.L.F. must win more people, intellectuals, doctors, teachers, not lose them. The strength of the N.L.F. comes from the fact that they form a front. I can't speak for the South, but we in the North appreciate the American intellectuals. And we cherish our own independence. This is only a sort of Western propaganda because they want to oppose the workers to the intellectuals, a fabrication.

"I want you to understand what is in our heart," Vy continued. "When we say we love peace, this is not a mere word. If it is not because of the interests of peace in Vietnam I would not have left my home in the South in 1954. This is why we used to say the situation under Diem and the United States has forced our people to come to such a course of struggle. This is why I said the whole significance of their struggle is that it is a struggle to exist, for the right to live. It is not because they are bellicose. The only conclusion is to guarantee peace, independence, and unity. Those are the fundamental things.

"We are confident that whatever the number of troops brought to Vietnam, the United States will not win. The fourteen million South Vietnamese people have enough knowledge, spirit, and determination to wage the struggle with their own efforts. They are able to limit most modern American weapons. The B-52, for instance, is not effective because the Southern people have a method of close hand-to-hand fighting. I will tell, for instance, the story of the spiked trench. United States troops need to be very mobile from their base to their target. However, at the last moment, they must go on foot at least five hundred meters. There are incalculable numbers of holes—trenches filled with spikes made of bamboo. They are impossible for modern electronics and radar to discover. The most effective way to discover our traps is to use poles and prods. But then the Americans cannot be quick and mobile. This explains why the United States only moved one kilometer in seven hours at Pleime. Guerrillas know the ground and can move around. It is impossible for a helicopter to land in a jungle; the same with a tank in a quagmire. Also the logistical support for guerrillas is simple, but the U.S. troops have very complicated requirements. We can solve questions on the spot, but the U.S. must bring equipment from the U.S. The Vietnamese population supports the guerrillas, helps fighters hide their secrets."

Tom asked about the relations of the three most widely known sects of South Vietnam—the Hoa Hao, Cao Dai, and Binh Xuyen—to the N.L.F. and Saigon. The Hoa Hao and Cao

Dai are primarily religious, though both have had their own armies; the Binh Xuyen was alleged to control much of the organized crime in the South, and also possessed its own military strength. Traditionally all three were anti-Communist, but after vicious repressions by Diem they seem to have become neutral or pro-N.L.F.

"The present situation is different than under the French. I think the U.S. lags behind in one point. The French succeeded in mobilizing these sects, but not the Americans. Fundamentally the three are peasant groups and are Vietnamese. They saw that it was not profitable to follow Diem. They know they won nothing from the French. Also they were considered traitors by the people. When someone is considered a traitor, a most terrible thing it is. Diem terrorized all those who opposed him. That, too, was important."

Tom asked why they followed the French in the past.

"They were told the Communists were against religion. But people know. They realize the N.L.F. is not against religion. The agents of the Americans are against religion. The N.L.F. has experience in building a front."

Then he concluded: "South Vietnamese people have their own methods of fighting. Many U.S. plans have failed. For instance, at the beginning the plan was to pacify South Vietnam in eighteen months. And then it was reduced to pacifying the key areas. At the beginning there was use of puppets without U.S. troops, now the U.S. adds its force to puppet troops. From bad to worse it goes. In the beginning the war was in the South, now in the North too. The problem is to get the U.S. to draw conclusions from the experience we have.

"What was new in 1965 was the growing support of the world's people. Frankly we must say our people are very enthusiastic at hearing of the movement in the United States.

We know your difficulties. Conditions in France were much easier. Nevertheless, the U.S. people are growing in protest. We are tremendously grateful. We have asked ourselves what it is that makes a man like Morrison burn himself—the holiness, the nobility of his death!"

10

REVOLUTION
AND VIOLENCE II:
AS WE SEE IT

I

The Vietnamese we met seemed the gentlest people we had ever known. Their war has two characteristics commonly associated with nonviolence: they seek to build a new society at the same time that they fight; and the future they envision includes their present antagonists (Vietnamese and American) as partners and brothers. The guerrillas' struggle, we came to feel, has strengthened the traditions of community and democracy which are rooted in Vietnamese history. Yet they find pacifism and Western freedoms difficult to understand. Our hosts in North Vietnam spoke of democracy while criticizing "obstinate elements" and "intellectuals with socialist form but capitalist content." They could not understand why anyone would refuse to fight for what they are convinced is a just and popular revolution defending itself against American aggression.

We share their conviction. And, therefore, we are left with a problem of synthesizing our own feelings about nonviolence and civil liberties with our experience in Vietnam. Is it possible to favor both nonviolence and anti-colonial revolution, civil liberties for all and the overthrow of the old social order?

The established Western description of revolution and revolutionaries fails us in Vietnam. The West says the revolutionist is one who sacrifices all the meaning of the present in behalf of an abstract future, an ideology, a total vision. Thus murder and terror are committed in the name of an unrealized justice; and revolutionaries are hardened, narrow, fierce, lacking all care for the decency that can be held and gained here and now. They are hungry only for power. The Asian revolutionary, the guerrilla, is seen as a mean little man, living like a beast off berries in the jungle, disemboweling villagers to terrify others, so feebly endowed with personal values that he can be the tortured or the torturer without flinching.

The revolutionaries we met, including guerrilla fighters, were people whose commitment to the future stemmed from their commitment to the present lives they lead and the longings that grow from those lives. When the guerrillas told us that despite "the bombing and strafing . . . life is developing" in the liberated areas, that "there are no very rich or very poor," that they help "each other with production," we began to understand the deep personal stakes that people have in the Resistance War. Men do not simply revolt out of utopian ambitions; they revolt because of anger at crimes beyond correction and because the seeds of their chosen life cannot grow in the society they encounter.

Just as it is inadequate to think of a diabolical Red Menace, it is inadequate to think of revolution as morally clean. The very nature of such a groping process, involving so many thousands of people, inevitably means that many destructive acts will occur. There will be personality conflicts and power struggles, factional bitterness will spill into personal relations, violence will be used against the revolution and by it, and revolutionaries will sometimes become in practice the opposite of what their dreams demand.

The Vietnamese revolution has not been pure. Innocent people have been killed. Decent men have been purged. Peasants and farmers have felt not only the repressions of colonialism but also the coercion of their fellows during the revolution. This brutality can be explained as a "necessary" part of resistance against the greater evil of foreign attack and rule. It can be explained, but not explained away, because actual men decide to perform the brutality, because actual men are responsible for it. If in a police state men decide to rebel, they also choose the form their rebellion takes. That these choices are conditioned by general events cannot change the fact that men deliberate over them, often in torment and struggle, and confronted with any particular decision have the option to say No.

We have to separate the idea of a genuine revolutionary force from the organizational practice or moral character of particular revolutionaries. There is a revolutionary force in Vietnam. It is simply the aspiration to rise above misery, because people have realized that misery is not inevitably their condition. Out of what Carl Oglesby calls "social desperation" arise a variety of protests, some individual and some collective, which become common, and, finally, a tradition. This body of experience is named "the movement" or "the revolution." In creating their tradition of protest, people discover what they need and what steps they must take to realize their needs. Petitioning and marching are used. So are political campaigns. Civil disobedience occurs. Workers and peasants strike. Students leave their books and take direct action. Organizations develop to express various currents: labor groups, peasant associations, parties, student movements. People learn what their own strength is and what resistance is being thrown up against them.

There is a mean side of the process. It is just as real as the more decent side, expressed in those moments when individuals overcome themselves, or people suddenly feel the deep emotional meaning of solidarity and community. We ought not to define revolution in terms of either its lowest or highest moments, but as an objective reality, a force that grips men: a force which men can somewhat shape, for better or worse, but never arbitrarily create or extinguish. We suggest this as an alternative to judging revolution either by the number of bodies disemboweled or by the humanism of its vision. The critics and partisans of the Vietnamese revolution too often take these paths, the critics identifying revolution with its terror and the partisans with its brotherliness.

In general, we believe in identifying with the revolutionary process and finding ways within one's limits to make it as humane as possible. But these are merely words: no formula can take the place of individuals personally struggling with the existential decisions involved. Were we in Vietnam, we imagine that we would support the National Liberation Front without surrendering the right to criticize and to decline to participate in particular actions. For Staughton, as a personal pacifist, this presumably would mean either noncombatant service in the Army of the Front (the capacity in which he served in the United States Army in 1953 and 1954) or alignment with one of the groups which operates separately from both the Front and the Ky Government. Tom feels perhaps a more direct identification with the National Liberation Front, especially the young organizers who build while they fight, without whom, he fears the revolution would be crushed and Vietnam made into an American colony. But the question is unreal since we are not in Vietnam. We find something artificial in the attitude of Americans who categorically condemn the Front's violence but have not themselves demonstrated that an alternative exists; we feel almost as distant from those who support the Front and all its works without comprehending that (in the words of Frantz Fanon) "no one takes the step of planting a bomb in a public place without a battle of conscience."[1]

[1] Frantz Fanon, *Studies in a Dying Colonialism*, p. 55.

Fanon himself is often invoked to justify the need and even desirability of violence in wars of national liberation. But the Algerian revolutionary and psychotherapist who died in 1961 at the age of thirty-six in fact took a position toward violence that was complex, agonized, and in process of development. True enough, his last book *The Wretched of the Earth* (New York, 1965) began with the assertion that "decolonisation is always a violent phenomenon" and dismissed nonviolence as "an attempt to settle the colonial problem around a green baize table" (pp. 29, 49). Violence, Fanon argued, also exorcises the native's personal sense of inferiority; breaks down the barriers between participants in the revolution by initiating them into a common, irreversible commitment; and serves to prevent the appearance of demagogic leaders after the revolution takes power, because its nature is direct and concrete.

But even in *The Wretched of the Earth*, Fanon the therapist had not lost sight of the psychological costs of violence. Thus he told of a patient, a revolutionary in his thirties, who suffered each year from "prolonged insomnia, accompanied by anxiety and suicidal obsessions" on the anniversary of the date on which he placed a bomb which killed ten people. The characteristic cause of the mental illnesses Fanon treated, whether of the tortured or the torturers, was "the bloodthirsty and pitiless atmosphere, the generalisation of inhuman practices" (pp. 205–206).

This sensitivity was more pronounced in Fanon's earlier work, published in English as *Studies in a Dying Colonialism*. It was here that he spoke of the battle of conscience the terrorist must suffer, and of planned acts of terror called off at the last moment for this reason. In the Preface to *Studies*, Fanon insisted that sudden acts of violence are "psychologically understandable," and are quantitatively insignificant compared to the violence of the colonizers. Yet he concluded that torture or the murder of women and children by revolutionaries must be condemned "with pain in our hearts," in order that the revolution will

In Algeria as described by Fanon, in Vietnam as described by Burchett, the decision to use terror was made reluctantly, after other methods had failed at terrible cost to break the iron grip of repression.

Conscious of the ferocity of both sides in the Vietnamese war, we were impressed by an absence of vengeful emotions and stereotyped hatreds among our hosts. Words most frequently said to us in Vietnam, by small children as by the Prime Minister, were: "We distinguish between the American people and the American Government." The distinction follows from Marxist ideology, which presupposes in the United States a potentially revolutionary populace restive under the rule of a governing class. Dogmatic as that conception may be, it has roots in the experience with their former French enemies, who finally came to harmony with the Vietnamese. The result of this orientation is an apparent absence of hatred toward Americans or white men as such. We anticipated resentment but felt it less than among Negroes in America. There was, however, evidence of bitter feelings under the warmth and optimism. Our young Vietnamese guides in Prague and Peking both possessed the cynical humor that often covers hate. The factory manager said the word "American" had become hard for the Vietnamese to hear. We have seen the transcript of an interview with a captured American pilot who was surprised (as was the pilot with whom we spoke in Hanoi) by the medical attention and generally adequate care he received, but who also mentioned that he had been moved from a particular village because of the hatred felt there about U.S. bombing. And, if China can be considered

---

not be the substitution of one "barbarism" for another. In the best tradition of nonviolence he asserted: "What we Algerians want is to discover the man behind the colonizer. . . . We want an Algeria open to all" (pp. 24, 25, 32).

comparable, our friend Tang warned of young people "going overboard" with bitterness. This was about all we encountered—unless our hosts' weeping should be interpreted as rage withheld—to suggest enmity toward Americans as a group. (Tom supposed this might be due to confidence drawn from their historical achievements, possibly making it easier for them to avoid the frustrating sense of self-doubt and inferiority which colonialism usually instills in the colonized.) Our guilt seemed greater than their hatred.

We recognized that our informants would have tended to repress whatever anti-American feelings they had in speaking to three American guests. We also are aware that the United States prides itself on the "measured" violence of its Vietnamese war-making, and that stereotypes which disparage whole peoples are less virulent in this war than in previous American contests with "the Huns" and "the Japs." But in our judgment what distinguishes Vietnamese from American violence is not a matter of motive so much as of objective context. Both sides use violence, but this does not mean both sides are equally violent. In the last analysis, the other side employs violence more discriminately, first, because it simply has less military hardware and is obliged to rely more on men; second, because it fights among its own people for a cause which enjoys more popular support than the cause sponsored by the United States.

II

Since the issue of terror is used by the American Government as the key to its rejection of "the other side," let us explain more fully why we cannot join in the conventional condemnation of Vietnamese revolutionaries as murderers. First of all, the violence of guerrillas is a reaction to the violence of life under colonial domination, a system that continued under Diem after the French left, and which continues after Diem under American auspices. Nearly all political channels are closed. In March, 1965, advocacy of peace was made a capital crime. The law was enforced by ten- to twenty-year sentences in August and by executions in September. In March, 1966, a group of experts assembled by the American Friends Service Committee noted wryly that the United States Government claims that its greater involvement has strengthened South Vietnamese will to win, "but such an effect is difficult to demonstrate because the present junta led by General Ky has outlawed as traitors all those who . . . even discuss the possibility of a peaceful settlement." Today, the Ky Government still forbids the candidacy of Communists and "neutralists," and as of August, 1966, held in jail—"most of them without having had any charges brought against them"—four to five thousand Buddhists, students, and soldiers thought to have opposed the Government the previous spring.[2]

This is the same pattern, in an extreme form, that appears in our own society when workers strike violently or Negroes rebel in a place like Watts. If such rebellion seems grim or excessive, in our opinion it is the landlords, officials, and police who make it so by blocking the channels of change.

Just as the N.L.F. and American terror spring from different furies, so also they are directed at different targets. Burchett quoted an N.L.F. guerrilla to the effect that assassination of village officials is directed only against particularly cruel administrators, and only after they are invited to stop working for the Saigon Government and have refused.[3] David Halber-

[2] *Peace in Vietnam,* p. 49; Robert Shaplen, "Letter From Saigon," *The New Yorker,* August 20, 1966, p. 124.

[3] Burchett, *Vietnam: Inside Story of the Guerilla War,* pp. 146–147.

stam, in *The Making of a Quagmire*, first stated that in 1960 the N.L.F. began systematically to eliminate bad and corrupt officials together with some unusually able ones, making a particular target of schoolteachers. "Again and again, the story was the same: brutal murders, decapitation of village officials and teachers in front of an entire village."[4] Subsequently, however, when Halberstam described not what was told him but what he himself observed in 1962–63, he gave this account:

When they [the Vietcong] attacked, they attacked only the symbols of the Government: the armory or command post of the hamlet, the hamlet chief or the youth leaders (who were particularly hated because they were Nhu's men). They rarely harmed the population, and so the people of a village, who saw that the Government had not kept its promises and could not protect them, often sided with the Vietcong after a raid.[5]

In this second passage, N.L.F. violence suggests not so much the "bandits" of United States propaganda as the assassination of Vichy collaborators by the French Resistance during World War II.[6]

The N.L.F. isolates and often kills persons who represent Saigon and the United States in the villages: typically, they are Catholic, urban-trained, much more affluent than the villagers, appointed from Saigon rather than elected by the people. They are not "innocent civilians" but salaried partisans in a war. When they are killed it is often to gain the confidence

[4] David Halberstam, *The Making of a Quagmire* (New York, 1965), pp. 64–65.

[5] *Ibid.*, p. 189. For a similar portrayal of N.L.F. terror, see Browne, *The New Face of War*, pp. 102, 104, 109.

[6] This analogy to the French Resistance was invoked by the veteran Japanese diplomat Shunichi Matsumoto in the *Asahi Evening News*, April 6, 1965, and a year later, by Bernard Fall in the Epilogue to his *Viet-Nam Witness*.

and support of the villagers, not to frighten them into silence. United States Special Forces personnel are trained to do the same thing for the same reason.[7]

In addition, the N.L.F. bombs restaurants, hotels, and other quarters in Saigon. Is this nothing more than terror against innocents? Again we would answer No, that the N.L.F. is using for its own purposes the American concept of "denying sanctuaries" to the enemy. If the Air Force bombs the jungle encampments where N.L.F. troops are resting, how is it different when the N.L.F. bombs the restaurants where its enemies relax?

It is this "no sanctuaries" kind of thinking that has been used to justify the Air Force's bombing of civilians all over Vietnam. But occasional N.L.F. bombing of gathering places for Americans is quantitatively different from routine bombing of villages because they are suspected of harboring the N.L.F. The fundamental reason American atrocities are larger in number is that we lack the confidence of the people. The N.L.F. lives basically among the people; Americans in Vietnam live surrounded by barbed wire. The N.L.F. practices selective terror on the ground; Americans—not because they are sadistic but because their Government is counterrevolutionary—rain indiscriminate terror from the skies. From one point of view (more compelling to Staughton than to Tom) it

[7] Former Sergeant Donald Duncan of the United States Special Forces stated that during the Green Berets' Fort Bragg training "killing unpopular officials is pointed out as one method of gaining friends among the populace." ("The Whole Thing Was a Lie," *Ramparts*, February, 1966, p. 21). If Robin Moore is right in asserting that *The Green Berets* is accurate, the training Duncan described is put into practice: "DePorta was slated for the first Batcat mission of the night: assassinating the new political officer. . . . The great value of assassinating political chiefs, DePorta had stressed, was that you hurt the central government without alienating the population." (Robin Moore, *The Green Berets* [New York, 1965], pp. 325–326).

is important to say that any act of terror is wrong: but it also is important to point out that the balance of terror is by no means even.

Our difference with our Government over the problem of terror blends into our difference over the problem of popular support. American planners deny the popular basis of the Vietnamese revolution; therefore, they say, terror must be the means by which Ho Chi Minh holds together his population. In a typical expression of this view, the veteran British diplomat Donald Lancaster, who was in Vietnam for years, wrote that the entire population in the North is "harassed, dragooned and deprived of all privacy and leisure."[8] That we failed to notice this "harassed, dragooned, and deprived" population while in North Vietnam will come as no surprise to critics who find the "massive tranquillity" of Hanoi "ominous."[9] For them, contented Communists must be slaves without guards. The fact that we saw no armed police in Hanoi is taken as evidence of a perfected tyranny, and we are advised to cast aside as mere propaganda the words of one Vietnamese who told us: "Our people hated police with clubs so much, after the years of French domination, that we vowed never to have them again."

The relative absence of police, we were told in Hanoi, leaves considerable power over neighborhood matters in the hands of elected "block committees." These committees, said the Vietnamese, try to solve local incidents by discussion or by referral to the courts. For Lancaster, this too is an ominous part of the totalitarian net. In his version of North Vietnamese society, the people are divided into "cells" of twelve members, each member being responsible for working with and criticizing the

[8] Lancaster, *The Emancipation of French Indochina*, p. 363.
[9] Fall, *Viet-Nam Witness*, p. 113.

other eleven. Each group rises at dawn "to the prospect of collective physical exercises." They meet together at least twice a week for self-criticism and discussion of issues and doctrines. "Their enslavement [is] completed by obligatory membership in one of the many associations founded on the possession of a common profession, sex, or age."[10] They also are required to do unpaid work on behalf of the community, such as building schools and bridges.

For Fall, too, the street committees constitute "an unofficial police force which plays on a man's desire to keep the Joneses down with him if he cannot keep up with them."[11] (The concept is apt, for an American official in Laos has described the purpose of American aid as "creating Joneses for people to keep up with." The United States aid program involves creation of artificial competitive incentives, the absence of which is presumed to be responsible for poverty.)

The same charge is brought against the N.L.F. A January 29, 1966, article in *The Saturday Evening Post*, "Under Viet Cong Control," began by telling how the N.L.F. goes door-to-door in the liberated zones "to enlist the voluntary support of the villagers." But the "liberation associations" formed in this way among farmers, women, youth, students, workers, and professionals, through which "weddings and burials are arranged, farmers are helped at harvest," are then characterized as a "VC mesh," which exercises "nearly total control."

There are other ways to interpret this reality in Vietnam. We have a parallel, if we would look at it, in our own history. The idea of small, face-to-face communities was common in nineteenth-century American society which, like Vietnam, was primarily rural. Oanh told us that Vietnam does not have a

10 *The Emancipation of French Indochina*, p. 363.
11 *Viet-Nam Witness*, p. 109.

problem of bureaucracy because "we are a small country." But everyone is a member of one or several organizations because we think that is the best guarantee of democracy, he added. A similar portrait of a society that can be organized but not bureaucratic will be found in the writings of the French critic De Tocqueville, who commented of nineteenth-century America that its web of voluntary associations was the basis of its democracy. Were those American associations so "voluntary" and the Vietnamese groupings so "compulsory" that they have nothing in common? We suspect that colonial American town meetings and current Vietnamese village meetings, Asian peasants' leagues and Black Belt sharecroppers' unions have much in common, especially the concept of a "grass-roots" or "rice-roots" democracy. Bernard Fall, no friend of the Hanoi Government, has quoted this bit of self-criticism from the November 24, 1962, edition of the Party newspaper *Nhan Dan:*

People's Council delegates have seldom acted as local representatives to go deeply into local economic, political, and cultural problems . . . to listen to the electors' views, to know their desires, and to get a clear idea of the people's conditions of life . . . these shortcomings have somewhat loosened the ties between the government and the people and between the electorate and their representatives, thus indirectly limiting the people's right as masters of the government.[12]

Whatever the quantity of coercion in the neighborhoods, villages, and other building blocks of society in "liberated" Vietnam, it can hardly be compared to the violence of the U.S.–sponsored strategic hamlet program of 1961–63. The French specialist Jean Lacouture commented:

[12] Fall, *The Two Viet-Nams,* p. 136.

By touching the villages Nhu [Diem's brother] and his friends touched at the very foundations of Vietnamese peasant culture, where the local group, bound in its bamboo collar, had remained the basic unit, the raw material of public life, and even the basis of private life. The village, even more than the individual, was an entity. It was the village that had to pay taxes, and the villages that negotiated with the central power. Everything derived from that entity, and all came down to it. It was the expression of that "harmony beneath the heavens" that any society imbued with Confucianism considered essential.[13]

Whereas North Vietnam (Professor Thong told us) seeks to build socialism on the basis of this traditional village communalism, the strategic hamlet program of the South was in Lacouture's words "more revolutionary than the Viet Minh." He said:

In this ancient country to jeopardize the village structure by setting up artificial agglomerations is to break the backbone of the country itself, to go against its collective conscience, its beliefs, and its homogeneity at the deepest level.[14]

There is no more shameful example of the double standard in American commentary on Vietnam than the facility with which scholars and journalists denounce the totalitarianism of the enemy but pass by our own brutality in the strategic hamlet program.

If Western critics are blind to these differences, the Vietnamese people surely are not. They know the difference between a traditional village and a strategic hamlet, and between what the U.S. and the "enemy" offer in other fields as

[13] Lacouture, *Vietnam: Between Two Truces*, p. 89.
[14] *Ibid.*, p. 158.

well. While a girl in North Vietnam spoke of education providing thousands of young people with "new wings," an Agency for International Development official said of South Vietnamese youngsters from Kienhoa province, where less than two in each thousand will finish high school: "To these children the Vietcong offers the only real outlet for their energy."[15] And Vietnamese peasants are not indifferent spectators of international diplomacy. They know that while the U.S. Government talks of peace, their rice crops are poisoned and their children bombed. Thich Nhat Hanh, a non-Communist Buddhist monk whose work as head of Youth for Social Service has taken him among the peasants of South Vietnam, stated in May, 1966, that "ninety percent of the peasants he has talked with regard President Johnson's peace moves as insincere."[16]

III

Western critics support their case against North Vietnam as a totalitarian state with references to political suppression and, above all, land reform. We were able to talk with Professor Thong about these issues, a rare opportunity. In addition we wish to offer our own observations and interpretation.

Speaking first of the killing of Ta Thu Thau and other Vietnamese Trotskyists after World War II, the professor said:

"In 1945 there were a number of regrettable events. Notable personalities were killed, among them a leader of the Vietnamese Trotskyists. But in fact there was no official policy of the Government. Sometimes they were killed by local author-

[15] *New York Times*, February 19, 1966.
[16] *Ibid.*, May 17, 1966.

ities or by aroused masses in localities. It was the high tide of revolution, and we often did not know how or why people were killed. I hope you understand."

Tom mentioned Camus' fear of victims becoming executioners. Thong said:

"The masses hated and killed people they considered pro-French. The Trotskyist leaders opposed the power of the revolution. At that time I was in France. I don't know exactly how it happened. But in France I had experience struggling with Trotskyists. I was in the D.R.V. office at that time and our duty was to unite with the French people to prevent war. But at that time French and Vietnamese Trotskyists fought against our Government. They said the Government made two mistakes. First, they opposed the policy of uniting the whole country, bourgeoisie and peasants, because they said it would annihilate the class struggle. So they accused the D.R.V. of the incorrect line, saying the class struggle was the first question for Marxists. Second, they did not want to have peace negotiations at that time [1945].

"Our objection to the Trotskyists was, if we fought against the French at that time, people might not understand it, and at the same time we were not prepared. This was right after the August revolution. We didn't have weapons, had just come to power. We also needed an explanation to the French people on our work. First we wanted peace and independence but to avoid war. We compromised. To some extent we achieved independence but not fully. We wanted independence but no weapons. We wanted to use, first, political means of action; second, unite our people; third, get support from the French people.

"The Trotskyists stood for war, not for unity of the people. They made no distinction between the French people and the French aggressors. We had to pay attention to the French people, make them understand Vietnam as a colonial country. If we had fought without explanation, they might have thought we were rebelling within France, the same as a state in the U.S. might ask for independence. After August, 1945, Ho invited Bao Dai into the Government. So was a bishop of the Vietnamese Catholic Church invited."

Tom asked: "We criticize Johnson for not protecting the lives of civil rights workers; why couldn't Ho protect the Trotskyists?"

"In South Vietnam there was a court convicting the head of a religious sect in South Vietnam. President Ho criticized the trial saying it would have been better for South Vietnam to send the man to him so that everything could be explained. Through our experience we see that when Ho talks, there is an impact on those who decide to listen. Ho never would decide to kill."

Professor Thong's approach seemed to us neither Leninist nor Buddhist but sounded more like the German socialist playwright Bertolt Brecht who brooded over the fact that "we who laid the foundations of kindness could not ourselves be kind" and asked future generations to "judge us not too harshly."

The best-known Western indictment against North Vietnamese Communism concerns the "agrarian reform" on the Chinese model carried out in 1954-56. Western sources give the following picture. Land reform committees organized community trials of well-to-do farmers, frequently followed by imprisonment or execution. Perhaps as many as fifty thousand to one hundred thousand persons were killed. Whatever the number, even Communist sources confessed many serious "errors" (Radio Hanoi, November 22, 1956), demoted officials responsible for the program, and abolished the land reform tribunals. There were rebellions in south-central North Vietnam, and notably in Ho Chi Minh's native province of Nghe An, where five thousand to ten thousand peasants were suppressed by Government troops.[17]

So far as we know, Professor Thong's comments on this somber episode represent the only direct response from "the other side" to Western charges concerning North Vietnamese agrarian reform.

"Reactionary Catholic leaders," said the professor, "took advantage of Catholic people to protest. They said cooperative ownership violated private ownership by the peasants. In some places, fanatic Catholic people protested against the policy. A number of land reform cadres were killed. Several people were arrested. They were not killed but sent to prison. It was not a big number except in a few places. Articles were printed in the North Vietnamese press which the West exploited. The intellectuals who wrote the articles still work for our Government but their jobs have been changed. Individuals in the Catholic Church are still opposed to land reform but not the Church itself."

Professor Thong insisted: "This was not suppression, just arrest by the police. To my knowledge, no one was killed." He went on: "We had this in our minds. The laboring people can understand things if explained to them; however, they can make mistakes. That is why we always treat prisoners very well, including foreigners. Africans imprisoned in 1946–54 often became leading revolutionaries." Staff Sergeant George E. Smith and Specialist Fifth Class Claude McClure, he reminded us in conclusion, had been released by the N.L.F., but

[17] See Lancaster, *The Emancipation of French Indochina*, pp. 377–378; Devillers in *Vietnam*, ed. Gettleman, p. 220; Fall, *Viet-Nam Witness*, pp. 96–104.

D.R.V. news reports said they were being held in Okinawa to be tried by their own Army.

How should one evaluate the conflicting accounts about agrarian reform in North Vietnam? We should like to urge caution in approaching this controversy. It is necessary to remember the tendency of Western media to seize on and exaggerate any crumb of information about the evils of Communism. It is also necessary to remember that a whole generation of Western radicals used this fact to blind themselves to the existence of other facts: arbitrary executions and forced labor camps in Stalin's Russia. We wish to comment on three or four points of the controversy, and tentatively suggest a way of conceptualizing the problem.

These things seem to us reasonably clear:

1. Fall and Thong agreed that Catholicism was involved in the Nghe An rising; Fall said the farmers concerned were "predominantly Catholic."[18]

2. Fall and Thong agreed that the events of 1956 involved discontent among North Vietnamese intellectuals as well as rural unrest.[19]

3. The event in Nghe An province was, in the words of Devillers, a "small peasant revolt."[20] The unreliability of even the best Western scholarship in such matters is suggested by the fact that in one essay Fall estimated the number of rebels as "perhaps 10,000," in another (written five years later) reduced the number to 6,000, while in a third place he stated: "allegedly, close to 6,000 farmers were *deported or executed* [authors' italics]."[21] If five to ten thousand people were involved, rather than killed or arrested, this would not be inconsistent with

---

18 *Viet-Nam Witness*, p. 101.
19 *Ibid.*, p. 103.
20 Devillers, *Vietnam*, ed. Gettleman, p. 220.
21 *Viet-Nam Witness*, pp. 101, 111; *The Two Viet-Nams*, p. 157.

Thong's statement that the number imprisoned was small "except in a few places."

4. Similar variation appears in Western estimates of the number killed during the land reform as a whole. Fall's estimate was fifty thousand to one hundred thousand deaths.[22] Lancaster said that in December, 1956, twelve thousand persons were released from forced labor camps and that "the number of those who had been murdered was unofficially estimated as between ten and fifteen thousand."[23] Jean Lacouture told us that French officials in Hanoi at the time gave him a figure lower still. Nevertheless, unless Professor Thong misunderstood our question to refer only to the Nghe An rising rather than to agrarian reform as a whole, there is a sharp contradiction between even the lowest Western estimate of deaths and his statement, "To my knowledge, no one was killed."

We suggest that this episode should be viewed as an extension of the war against the French, and the violence involved should be assessed in the same context as the terror of the Resistance itself.[24] The agrarian reform program which culminated in the 1956 rebellion had in fact been adopted in 1953 while the war was still in progress. The land policy of the Vietminh went through two stages. The first phase began in June, 1949, when Ho stated that landlords who cooperated with the Resistance would not be disturbed; but land would be

[22] *Viet-Nam Witness*, p. 124.
[23] *Emancipation of French Indochina*, p. 377.
[24] Since these summary paragraphs were written, the argument they present also has been offered by Neil Sheehan. He said that when the Vietminh accelerated its land reform program in 1953, Emperor Bao Dai decreed a reduction of rents "from the traditional 40 to 50 per cent of the rice crop to 15 per cent" in order "to compete with the Vietminh." The landlords refused and the Vietminh triumphed. Since 1953 the Americans have replaced the French, "yet among the Vietnamese themselves, the two opposing sides have changed little." (*New York Times Magazine*, October 9, 1966).

confiscated from the French settlers, or the French companies, or those native landlords who betrayed the Resistance or fled the liberated areas, Starobin reported. "The Republic also proceeded to divide the communal lands where it could," and "by the middle of 1952, one hundred thousand acres had been allotted to more than 420,000 peasants,"[25] he continued. Related measures decreed a 25 percent reduction in rents and a reduction of interest rates to 18 to 20 percent.

The second stage of the program began in 1953 when more emphasis was put on the anti-feudal, social revolutionary side of the Vietminh program. The new policy stipulated: "Landowners whose record in the Resistance was a good one were to be compensated by state bonds, but they had to give up all land beyond that which was necessary for their own livelihood. Landlords who resisted this reform, or who had records as 'despots' and had committed crimes against the people, were liable to five years' imprisonment." Starobin added that this decision was made during his visit to the jungle and was prompted in part by "dissatisfaction among the peasants with the behavior of many landlords and with the slow process of agrarian change."[26]

This version of the genesis of North Vietnamese land reform is indirectly corroborated by the process of land reform in the "liberated" areas of South Vietnam today. Peter Grose of the *New York Times* wrote on January 24, 1965:

Unencumbered by any responsibilities of the past the Vietcong stake much of their appeal in the hamlets on giving out land to the people who work it. Previous titles of absentee landlords are swept aside and the land is ceremonially parcelled out to the peasant families.

[25] *Eyewitness in Indo-China*, p. 87.
[26] *Ibid.*, p. 90; Bernard Fall, *The Viet-Minh Regime* (New York, 1956), described the 1949–53 decrees in detail.

Just as in North Vietnam, so in liberated South Vietnam the village as a whole determines the redistribution of land. Grose continued:

When disputes arise among farmers, the parties argue their cases before a hamlet meeting until one side withdraws before a consensus judgment of his neighbors guided by the Vietcong administrator, who may also act as arbiter. Only as a last resort is force used against recalcitrant individuals who may be summarily executed as examples.

On the other hand, in N.L.F.-controlled South Vietnam now as in North Vietnam in 1954–56 the revolution may push forward land reform too quickly, relying too much on force rather than the development of a "mass base." In July, 1962, the United States Information Service released a document entitled _Experiences in Turning XB Village in Kien Phong Province into a Combatant Village_, the original of which had been taken from a captured member of the Front.[27] Its anonymous author explained that land reform in this village of "one big landowner and 50 smaller ones" was the basis of N.L.F. activity there. But at first, he said, the Party "began the elimination of influence of the village notables and local security agents" without "the development of a mass base." Realizing its error, a meeting was called at which the peasants were warned "that if the American-Diem clique succeeded in permanently maintaining the organization of village notables and security soon Mister H. the cruel landlord and others would return to the village to seize land and collect back rent." A successful program developed, the Front simultaneously urg-

[27] This document is reprinted in _Vietnam_, ed. Robin Murray _et al._ (London, 1965), pp. 81–88, and discussed by Warner in _The Last Confucian_, pp. 143–151.

ing the notables and their families to come over to the side of the people while urging the people to rise up and eliminate the influence of the notables.

This is the process we think began in North Vietnam while the Resistance War was still being fought, at a time when (in Starobin's words) "the news that a change in the land system [was coming] with the approach of Ho's armies [was] unquestionably one of the strongest weapons in their military advance." Much the same process went on in 1946–54 in the South. Vy told us: "The people of South Vietnam very eagerly desire independence because they already had independence during the Resistance [against the French]. The peasants had land; they cannot stand it when it is taken." Not only was land theirs, but people throughout Vietnam knew that in 1945–46 Ho's revolutionary Government, in the words of historian Ellen Hammer, had "succeeded in doing what the French had not always been able to do: they had saved the country from famine by the unaided efforts of their citizens."[28] In both North and South Vietnam, the land reform program of the Vietminh appears to have had strong popular support.

Against this historical backdrop the American land reform program should be compared and reviewed. The plans brought to South Vietnam by American aid experts represent a policy of quite literal counterrevolution. The American dream was to develop an independent middle class of small farmers. The only extensive distribution of land, however, was to the Catholic, pro-French refugees who came down from the North in 1954. Not only did they receive land to cultivate, but they also received millions of dollars worth of technical assistance from the United States—a subsidy to a group which had opposed the national revolution. The plan for the rest of the country

28 Ellen J. Hammer, *The Struggle for Indochina* (Stanford, 1954), p. 146.

people, who were mainly Buddhists, included rent control programs, a ceiling on the number of hectares of land which could be individually owned, and some redistribution to be accomplished by purchasing land from large owners and reselling it on a long-term basis to would-be entrepreneurs. The problem built into this program was much deeper than all the corruption which distorted it. The problem was that Saigon and the United States were in fact renewing the ownership rights of landlords who had fled the countryside ten years earlier, letting them return to collect back rent from peasants who had taken over the land for themselves during the Resistance War. In this context, the ideas of rent control, ceilings, and the like missed the basic question of ownership, and turned the United States and Saigon governments into the enemy of the masses of country people.

We think that Saigon's betrayal of the peasant's hope for land is a major reason for its lack of popular support. Stanley Andrews, former director of United States technical aid to underdeveloped countries, who visited South Vietnam as a consultant three times between 1960 and 1965, stated in April, 1966, that "well-intentioned land reform programs . . . benefited refugees from North Vietnam and moderately well-to-do individuals . . . but not the peasants," and that in consequence "Vietnamese villagers expressed little support . . . for the Saigon government."[29] This also was the conclusion of a New York *Herald Tribune* reporter who observed that of the five classes in the Vietnamese countryside—landowners, rich peasants, middle-class peasants (those who own all their land but do not rent any to others), tenant farmers, and farm laborers—"an estimated 30 percent of the Viet Cong strength recruited in the South are considered to belong to the 'farm labor class.' " The *Herald Tribune* of June 3, 1965, reported:

[29] *New York Times,* April 30, 1966.

"The question of land reform is quite simple," one low-ranking Vietnamese provincial official explained. "The government represents the landowners; the ministers and generals are either landowners or friends of landowners. The Catholic Church owns land. The Buddhist Church owns land. Nobody is interested in fighting for the poor peasant. And the top Americans—well, they talk to only the ministers and rich people so they don't push it either."

Thus in both North and South Vietnam the drive for reform in the countryside, however cruelly and mistakenly executed, appears to have originated in wartime in response to the needs of the rural poor. We are conscious that too many Communist excesses have been rationalized on grounds of "capitalist encirclement" and wartime emergency. Yet it can be said of both the Vietminh and the N.L.F. that land reform was the necessary step that they had to take in order to win the peasantry and so win the war; or as Robert Scigliano puts it, in Vietnamese guerrilla war "the peasantry is not so much a pawn or a prize as it is the arbiter in the struggle."[30] We suspect that this is the right context in which to view the agony of land reform in all of Vietnam.

IV

We are not arguing that First Amendment liberties thrive in North Vietnam, and we do not believe we are Sartres who require a Camus to remind us of the existence of slave labor camps.

Because their society is in a life-and-death struggle, the North Vietnamese accept more direction and discipline than we in our more flexible society would be prepared to tolerate. The Vietnam war is marginal to us, but primary for them. We

[30] *South Vietnam: Nation Under Stress,* p. 159.

found somewhat spine-chilling Oanh's remark that certain dissident intellectuals had been "socialist in form but capitalist in content"; yet we believe that the great majority of North Vietnamese consider the martial law of a besieged fortress appropriate to their situation, and do not regard their Government as an oppressive tyranny. As we see it, Americans must learn to live with the ambiguity that the Government of Communist North Vietnam places many restrictions on the lives of its citizens but that it also seems to most of these citizens that they live in a freer society than they did under the French. Our guess would be that their contact with advocates of "pure" civil liberties has been primarily with those defending unjust privilege: French colonialists, landlords, wealthy Catholics, hypocritical Americans. After the war, when peaceful construction becomes possible, we hope the North Vietnamese will be open to contact and dialogue with radical Americans whose commitment to civil liberties masks no class or military motive, and that our two cultures will grow closer together as a result. For the present, if the United States is genuinely concerned to promote freedom for the North Vietnamese, it should stop bombing them.

We protest the tacit assumption of American policy-makers that when a country is "lost" to Communism the change is wholly away from freedom, and that the country concerned then becomes qualitatively so different from the "free" societies of the West that any measures are justified to prevent a Communist take-over. This is the premise which enables a Johnson or McNamara, after ordering the napalm bombing of women and children, to sleep at night. Staughton was one of a group of five pacifists who met with McNamara at his Pentagon office in June, 1965, and were told by him that he cared as much about men's souls as about their bodies. It took a few minutes for the group to realize that this was the Secretary's way of saying it is better to be dead than Red.

Readers may conclude fairly that our view of North Vietnamese life differs absolutely from that of the American Establishment. True as this is, we think it perhaps also possible that many powerful Americans would be in considerable agreement with our version of reality were it not so politically embarrassing. Throughout the past decade there have been repeated hints in official or prestigious circles that the Vietnamese Communists are not as evil as the stereotype suggests. Take these for example:

I would like to be able to report—I had hoped to be able to report—that on that long, slow canal trip to Vinh Binh (Mekong Delta), I saw all the signs of misery and oppression that have made my visits to East Germany like nightmare journeys to 1984. But it was not so. . . . At first it was difficult to conceive of a Communist government's genuinely "serving the people." I could hardly imagine a Communist government that was also a popular government and almost a democratic government. But this is just the sort of government the palm-hut state actually was while the struggle with the French continued. The Vietminh could not possibly have carried on the resistance for one year, let alone nine years, without the people's strong, united support.

Joseph Alsop, *New Yorker*, June 25, 1955, pp. 36, 48.

. . . the Communists have let loose a revolutionary idea in Vietnam and . . . it will not die by being ignored, bombed or smothered by us.

Major-General Edward Lansdale (the "Ugly American"),
Foreign Affairs, October, 1964, p. 76.

Even Premier Ky told this reporter today that the Communists were closer to the people's yearnings for social justice and an independent life than his own government.

James Reston, *New York Times*, September 1, 1965.

For years now in Southeast Asia, the only people who have been doing anything for the little man—to lift him up—have been the Communists.

Ambassador Henry Cabot Lodge, *New York Times*,
February 27, 1966.

This suggests to us that the American Government is in Vietnam because it believes that the spread of socialism is impermissible regardless of how humane the particular socialism involved. Underlying that belief, in turn, is the premise that everyone in the world, down deep, wants to live as white America lives. Everyone wants a little land, a little house, a few gadgets, the chance to enter the free market and make himself a giant corporation. In order to insure this for the world's people, the United States is prepared to borrow revolutionary techniques (as if they could be unharnessed from revolutionary goals). Our generals, intellectuals, and technicians read Lenin, Mao, Che Guevara, Vo Nguyen Giap; social scientists apply for grants to study "counter-insurgency" for the Defense Department; and the result is a pragmatic plan to use local armies in the "underdeveloped" countries to root out and kill the agitators, protect the innocent villagers, and pacify them with social and economic reform under military auspices.

American officials do not resort to wanton murder because they are bad or sadistic human beings. The problem lies in their assumption that in the long run a humane and free society must be based on private property under white American influence. It follows from this assumption that the grimmest political dictatorship is acceptable so long as private property remains, for if the undergirding institutional environment is "sound," temporary political trends can be reversed. It also follows from this assumption that if the small-scale violence of domestic dictatorship fails to stop Communism, the larger violence of war should be invoked. If the further assumption is made that all Communist-led revolutions today are planned in Peking, the theory provides no rational limit at which violence should stop.

It is this American strategy for the Third World which is responsible for America's increasing violence toward the impoverished human beings who inhabit it: for the strategy gravitates toward failure, failure induces frustration and desperation, and from these emotions springs violence. Because America fears social movements which attack private property and insist on economic planning, American aid programs support the most conservative of reforms: some literacy projects, some cooperatives, some agricultural equipment distributed, all administered through local politicians or the army. Such reforms barely scratch the surface of Third World misery, and accordingly fail. A revolutionary force develops in a pattern which should by now be familiar to us. With each stage of its growth the American predilection grows to scrap all talk and send in the Marines.

The pattern is something like this. Reactionary landholding and capitalist groups oppose all significant social reform while relying, first, on terror to maintain order and, second, on anti-Communist ideology to woo American support. In the middle are social reformers—usually urban, either trade unionists, intellectuals, or professional politicians—seeking to break the grip of reaction on their society but unwilling to base themselves in a revolutionary movement of workers and peasants. As these reform groups become popular, they arouse the hostility and fears of the oligarchy while at the same time failing to act with sufficient militancy to build mass support. The middle ground is hit by earthquake. The reformer must turn toward revolution, or retreat back into conservatism through the army or old parties and let the moving forces pass him by.

When non-Communist leadership turns toward fundamental change, such as basic land reform or the nationalization of foreign investments, American pressure mounts to destroy it. While American Peace Corpsmen and aid officials ply their Sisyphean labors in the villages, other Americans work among the oligarchs and generals to prevent a radical force from emerging. The reformer falls. The result finally is a revolutionary movement which opposes both reaction and reform.

The "domino theory" which should most concern us is the accumulating rage of American policy-makers as this cycle runs its course in one underdeveloped country after the other. Whatever happens in Vietnam, indigenous revolutionary forces on the one hand and the familiar American blindness on the other are preparing a similar drama on other Southeast Asian stages. *Crisis,* the newsletter of the Madison, Wisconsin, Committee to End the War in Vietnam, pointed out in its May 3, 1966, issue that we already have begun to misinterpret political conditions in Thailand. The newsletter compared two articles: Seymour Topping's "Next on Peking's Hit Parade?," published in the *New York Times Magazine,* February 20, 1966, and Alex Campbell's "Thailand: Is This Something To Fall Back On?," published in the *New Republic,* March 26, 1966. Whereas Topping, *Crisis* observed, "feels that the social and political unrest in Thailand would probably go away if the 'Communists' from Hanoi, Laos, and China would quit rabble-rousing," Campbell made the following points.

1. In the blighted Northeast region where annual peasant incomes run less than half the national average, the Bangkok regime has made some effort to improve social conditions through Mobile Development Units. But the effort has "flopped badly" because its administrators are viewed by the peasants as tax-collectors and "have a bad habit of calling the

peasants to their faces filthy, uncivilized pigs, making them squat on the ground in their presence, and making them call any policeman 'master.' "

2. Freedom of press, assembly, speech, and political parties, and the National Assembly, have been outlawed since 1959. Students and intellectuals (whom Topping said "have no taste for Communism") are beginning to murmur.

3. Whereas Topping accepted at face value Bangkok's identification of all discontent as "Communist," Campbell observed that Thai authorities for years have "described almost any armed person they nab as being a 'Communist terrorist' " with the purpose of playing on the United States paranoiac fear of Communism and thus keeping "the fighting in Vietnam and the dollars in Thailand."

Understandably, Topping followed the conventional domino theory and concluded that the "future of Thailand is being decided on the battlefields of Vietnam." But Campbell asked: "How would the U.S. feel about elections in Thailand that resulted in a civilian Thai government with a somewhat more independent, less mechanically anti-Communist policy? Already the U.S. is toying with the idea of falling back on Thailand if things go worse in Vietnam." In fact, by early 1966 there were more American troops in Thailand than there had been in Vietnam in early 1965.

Thus the American response to revolutionary peoples becomes our revolutionary technology. If that technology cannot be used to develop their societies on our terms, it will be used to threaten and, if necessary, destroy their societies. The modern revolutionary says people are the prime historical force; the technocrat, finger at the button, denies it. The guerrilla with his bamboo stick is opposed, finally, by the computer and SAC bomber.

11

WE ARE NOT AT WAR

"We must become internationalists again. For us, today, this means that we, personally, must refuse to fight the Cold War; that we, personally, must attempt to get in touch with our opposite numbers in all countries of the world—above all, those in the Sino-Soviet zone of nations. With them we should make our own separate peace."[1]

I

There was and is a question as to how the United States Government will respond to our trip. Nothing happened upon our arrival at Kennedy Airport except that Customs temporarily confiscated a variety of articles—*Selected Works of*

---

[1] C. Wright Mills, "The Decline of the Left," *Power, Politics and People: The Collected Essays of C. Wright Mills,* ed. Irving L. Horowitz (New York, 1963), p. 235.

Ho, several unused tapes, an appeal from Vietnamese to American Christians—from Tom's suitcase. Two days later, January 11, the Deputy Director of Far Eastern Research for the State Department flew to New Haven at the department's request to interview Staughton for two hours about our findings. Still nothing was said about passport violations.

Then on February 2, two days after the resumption of bombing became public knowledge, the department announced that it was "temporarily withdrawing" our passports. The reason, it was said, was that we had acted in a manner "prejudicial to the orderly conduct of foreign relations" and "prejudicial to the interests of the United States." For the moment at least the department had chosen to proceed by administrative reprisal rather than by legal prosecution.

Whether or not this action was constitutional is still unclear. Every United States passport states: "This passport is not valid for travel to or in Communist controlled portions of China, Korea, Viet-Nam, or to or in Albania, Cuba." In the 1965 Zemel Case, the Supreme Court upheld 6 to 3 the power of the department not to validate a passport for these or similarly proscribed countries. What the Supreme Court has not yet decided is whether or not the department has the power to punish persons who go to unauthorized countries without passport validation. And a 1966 decision in a lower federal court held that the department had no legislative mandate to control travel at all.

Fundamental issues are at stake in our cases. For one thing, as our attorneys of the American Civil Liberties Union observe, rather than punishing us for a trip to Hanoi the department is practicing "prior restraint upon future activities." Thus Staughton was prevented until the last moment from confirming acceptance of speaking invitations in non-prohibited countries such as England and Norway, evidently because the department thought that if he went to one of these states he might continue to China or Vietnam.

A more basic question is that of free speech. As the *New York Times* noted editorially on February 9, 1966, "in a free society newspapermen, professors and many other private citizens are meddling in foreign affairs all the time." We particularly were dismayed when on March 24, 1966, at the administrative hearing which the department's procedures provide, the Passport Officer stated on behalf of the department that speeches Staughton made in Washington on January 24 and Montreal on February 18 were among the Government's reasons in arguing that our passports should not be returned. When it was called to the Passport Officer's attention that Staughton had said nothing in Montreal about the trip to Hanoi, he responded that had it not been for the trip Staughton would not have been asked to speak! "It is the contention of the department in all such cases," the Passport Officer continued, "that the entire picture [including] activities subsequent to and growing out of" a trip are pertinent to the issuance or denial of a passport.

Thus, little as we anticipate travel abroad and disinclined as we both are to center our attention on travel rather than peace, the right to free contact between peoples—even of countries which do not have diplomatic relations—has come to seem to us an important symbol of the kind of world we hope to create. In any case, men of the second half of the twentieth century must learn to weigh the demands of their respective nation-states against the claims of world citizenship, as the judgment of the Nuremberg Tribunal directs. But especially in time of war and chronic Cold War, it seems vital that persons as well as governments be able to encounter one another directly. Freedom of travel expresses in action the spirit of Dwight D. Eisenhower's words of August 31, 1959: "I like to believe that the people in the long run are going to do more to promote peace than our Government. I think that the people want peace so much that one of these days governments had better get out of their way and let them have it."

Seen in this perspective, the right to travel becomes an aspect of the right of ordinary people to have some control over how they die.

To make war the modern administrator requires stereotypes. But if one can talk to people directly those stereotypes may crumble. Our personal experience, for example, was to observe a museum director, an interpreter, a factory manager—a variety of persons in official capacities—cry in public as they tried to describe the suffering of their country. This does not mean that all North Vietnamese officials cry in public. It means that they are neither faceless Communists nor inscrutable Orientals, that their feelings are as close to the surface as our own, that we should and must respond to their experience as if they were our own brothers and sisters.

Nuclear war would be inconceivable without a process of Cold War conditioning that begins with the refusal to "recognize" regimes which the American Government does not like and ends with the stereotyped view of an unknown "enemy." Freedom of travel is essential so that Americans can discover if in reality they have, in the words of Cassius Clay, "anything against them Vietcong."

II

When we say that our highest loyalty is not to America but to mankind, we affirm a lost part of the American tradition. Debs quoted Paine and Garrison when he went to jail to protest World War I, declaring: "My country is the earth and I am a citizen of the world." In 1846, Thoreau said, "This people must cease to hold slaves and to make war on Mexico, though it cost them their existence as a people," and insisted that Americans be "men first and Americans at a late and convenient hour."

The political philosophy of the Declaration of Independence takes as its point of departure universal human rights, and it resists total identification with any institutional framework. It is the distinctively American dream that all governments should be subordinated to rights which governments did not create; and that there are certain things—such as burning little children to death with napalm, or sentencing to hard labor writers who speak out against government policies—which must not be tolerated in any society under any circumstances.

Consider once more the familiar words of the preamble to the Declaration of Independence. What does "inalienable" mean? It does not mean that liberty cannot be taken away from you; rather it means the far more radical proposition that you cannot give up liberty. From the standpoint of the Declaration of Independence, men do not surrender their rights in becoming part of society. They create governments to "secure these rights." Representatives, trustees for the rights of their constituents, cannot give up their power of trusteeship: were Congress to make the President a dictator, the Declaration of Independence would render the act null. Still less can representatives give away the underlying individual rights which it is their duty to secure: were Congress and a requisite number of state legislatures duly to abolish the First Amendment, from the standpoint of the Declaration of Independence the action would have no effect upon the rights of man. These come not from Congress but from man's Creator, and "among" them—there presumably are others which the Declaration does not pause to enumerate—are life, liberty, and the pursuit of happiness. Thus Jefferson wrote to Frances W. Gilmer on June 7, 1816: "Our legislators are not sufficiently apprized of the rightful limits of their power; that their true office is to declare and enforce only our natural rights and duties, and to take none of them from us. . . . The idea is quite unfounded, that on entering into society we give up any natural right."[2]

According to the Declaration, the rights of man are not only "inalienable" but "self-evident." This does not mean that any two lawyers will agree about them; but the far more radical proposition that common men, using "common sense," can recognize and interpret their rights without the help of lawyers. The Declaration's stance on rights may seem a little distant and archaic to us because it is clothed in the language of natural law, and part of a theory of social contract which we find unusable. Let us then redefine the rights of man in the language of those men of the twentieth century who have sought to combine the most militant action on behalf of the oppressed with the affirmation that each human life is precious. Let us consider a "right" to be something held to be desirable by ancient ethical consensus, something not given man by social artifice but in him by virtue of the fact of being human.

The Declaration of Independence is not part of the United States Constitution and has no authority in an American court of law. Yet in our day its philosophy has begun to acquire legal form and weight. Justice Jackson and his colleagues at Nuremberg made it clear that if one presumes to create ex post facto law, the least one can do is to affirm that in the future this law will apply to oneself as well.

Consider some of the existential situations—among them

[2] *The Writings of Thomas Jefferson*, ed. Paul Leicester Ford, X (New York and London, 1899), p. 32.

freedom of travel—in which the rights of man as man proclaimed by the Nuremberg Tribunal and the Declaration of
Independence currently encounter the nation-state.

You are a young man of draft age. You have heard of the
Nuremberg Tribunal. You get a copy of its findings and read
its definitions of "war crimes" and "crimes against humanity."
You find in *Time* magazine for August 6, 1965, the twentieth
anniversary of the bombing of Hiroshima, the statement on
page 29 that "the Marines have begun to kill prisoners." You
read of the spring, 1965, decree of the Ky Government which
makes neutralism a capital offense.[3] You note that under this
decree three men, including a Saigon lawyer, were sentenced
to ten to twenty years' hard labor in August, 1965, and in
September of that year three other men were tied to posts on
the Da Nang soccer field and shot. Bearing in mind the
Nuremberg definition of "wanton destruction of cities, towns
or villages" as "war crimes," and "inhumane acts committed
against any civilian population" as "crimes against humanity,"
you read Father Currien's account of the bombing of a village
in South Vietnam by United States planes which, he said, struck
without warning at a time when no one was in the village but
"women, children and old people," and in contradiction to the
explicit statement of a ground troop commander, "You and

[3] The decree designated as treasonable engaging in "all direct or
indirect actions aimed at spreading Communist policies, slogans and
instructions by any individual or group of individuals influenced or controlled by the Communists," "all moves which weaken the national anti-
Communist effort and are harmful to the anti-Communist struggle of
the people and the Armed Forces," "all plots and actions under the false
name of peace and neutrality according to a Communist policy," "the
diffusion, circulation, distribution, sale, display in public places, and the
keeping of these above mentioned aims, either in printed form, drawings,
photographic, or otherwise." It also specified that "all associations,
agencies, and organizations violating [the aforementioned] shall be dis-
banded and their properties confiscated."

your faithful are no longer in danger." Then, if you are Norman Morrison, you drive from Baltimore to Washington that same afternoon and burn yourself to death.

If you are not Norman Morrison, you try to understand your obligations under the international law of the Nuremberg Tribunal. Suppose torture and murder of prisoners are exceptional acts by United States servicemen. Does that mean that you should enter the armed services, and refuse to commit such action only at the moment you are personally ordered to carry it out? Suppose saturation bombing of unprotected villages, either on suspicion of Vietcong presence or because the village is in a "free zone" where pilots may unload their bombs at will, is routine. Does that mean you should refuse participation in the war at the point of induction, or only that you should refuse participation in the Air Force? Suppose you are a draft-age young man but are not a member of an historic pacifist church. You would have fought in World War II. Were it possible for you to serve in a nonviolent capacity in Vietnam, offering medical aid, relief and reconstruction, or assistance in social revolution, you would gladly do it. Yet everything in you objects to this particular war. Three U.S. Army privates (the "Fort Hood Three") decided after their induction that the Vietnam war was unjust, illegal, and immoral. When they refused an order to board a plane for Vietnam, they were sentenced to three to five years in Army prisons.

You are a teacher who has such concerned young men in your class. Have you no obligation, or does the Nuremberg Tribunal indirectly impose on you the task of protesting against war crimes and crimes against humanity? Does your citizenship in a country committing such actions require you, not merely to say No, but to become as best you can a peacemaker? Further, you give grades which will be forwarded by the administration of your university to the Selective Service System. You are troubled, to use the language of a group of teachers at the University of Chicago, "about the effects on the educational process which may flow from linking students' classroom performance to their chances for induction," "by the notion that students deserve special preference with respect to selective service, or that academic performance should be a basis for distributing special privilege," "by the fact that this use of grades converts the University quite explicitly into an arm of the Selective Service System," and "by the fact that, by permitting our grades to be used in this way, we are actively cooperating in a war effort whose purposes we profoundly oppose." This group of teachers concluded "that the freedom of conscience of faculty and students who are opposed to the war effort" is violated by the Selective Service System's use of academic grades as a basis for induction and deferment. Is this a legitimate invocation of conscience? If a university were to fire a faculty member who refused to send in grades could he be defended under the First Amendment?

You are an American Negro. You know that young Negroes compose the group most exposed to the draft. No explanation quite makes it clear to you why the percentage of Negroes among American casualties in Vietnam is significantly higher than their percentage in the population. In the SNCC newsletter you read Charlie Cobb's poem:

> so cry not just
> for jackson or reeb
> schwerner, goodman
> or chaney
> or lee
>
> cry for all mothers
> with shovels

> *digging at hovels*
> *looking for their dead*
> *cry for all the blood spilled*
> *of all the people killed*
> *in the Standard Procedure*
> *of the country*
> *which is not ours*
> *but belongs*
> *to those who run it*
> *and can't be seen*
> *but are very few*
> *who*
> *listen to each other*
> *and not to us*
> *cause we don't know*
> *what it takes*
> *that makes*
> *Standard Procedure.*

You find a poem by Mrs. Ida Mae Lawrence, a leader of the striking laborers from the Mississippi delta who sought to occupy the Air Force base at Greenville and erected tents in Lafayette Park opposite the White House. It reads in part:

What does we have against the Vietnams?
Why are we fighting them?
Who are really the enemy?
Are Vietnam the enemy or we Americans enemies to ourselves?
If we are the same as Vietnams why should we fight them?
They are poor too.
They wants freedom.

If you live in McComb, Mississippi, where the SNCC voter registration drive began in autumn, 1961, you are disturbed when a young man active in that effort is drafted, sent to Vietnam, killed, and sent home in a coffin. You take part in drafting the statement of August, 1965: "1. No Mississippi Negroes should be fighting in Vietnam for the White Man's freedom, until all the Negro People are free in Mississippi. 2. Negro boys should not honor the draft here in Mississippi. Mothers should encourage their sons not to go. . . ."

As we flew back from Hanoi we read of the murder of SNCC worker Samuel Younge and of the SNCC staff's unanimous statement on the war. The first sentence asserted the right to dissent: "The Student Nonviolent Coordinating Committee assumes its right to dissent with United States foreign policy on any issue, and states its opposition to United States involvement in the war in Vietnam." Having asserted the right, the committee exercised it. The statement ends:

We are in sympathy with and support the men in this country who are unwilling to respond to the military draft which would compel them to contribute their lives to U.S. aggression in the name of the "freedom" we find so false in this country. . . .

We ask: Where is the draft for the freedom fight in the United States? . . .

We believe that work in the civil-rights movement and other human relations organizations is a valid alternative to the draft. We urge all Americans to seek this alternative, knowing full well that it may cost them their lives, as painfully as in Vietnam.

Within days the problem of conscience blended into the problem of self-government as Representative-elect Julian Bond was unseated. What part of the Constitution is applicable? The First Amendment? Or the guarantee of republican government?

You are a young man or woman and a socialist. The Attorney General of the United States asks the Subversive Activities Control Board to designate the W. E. B. DuBois Clubs of America as a Communist front. He knows that the

Supreme Court has ruled that individual members of organizations so designated cannot be required to register with the Government. He himself has recommended the repeal of the law under which he acts. Yet he does act, and the immediate consequence is hooliganism in Brooklyn and dynamiting in San Francisco. What bearing has the First Amendment here? In *W. E. B. DuBois Clubs of America v. Katzenbach*, Norman Thomas, the Reverend William S. Coffin, and other plaintiffs are seeking to enjoin the Attorney General from further proceedings under the McCarran Act "since free expression—of transcendent value to all society and not merely to those exercising their rights—will be the victim." In August, 1966, the House Un-American Activities Committee held hearings on anti-war activity during which an American Civil Liberties Union lawyer was physically dragged from the chamber as he tried to defend his clients.

You are not a draft-age young man, a professor, a Negro, or a socialist. You are an American citizen and taxpayer who happens to fall into none of these categories. You probably voted in November, 1964, for a Presidential candidate who had pledged himself not to "go North" and not to involve American troops in an Asian land war. Three months later, in a situation that was not an emergency, disregarding peace overtures from the other side, making no appeal to the United Nations, without an explanation to the public, and without a congressional declaration of war, he did what during the campaign he had said he would not do; and having done it, puts the blame for prolonging the war on those who criticize his action. What is the constitutional remedy for this situation?

Several hundred Americans, including professors at Columbia, Hofstra, Michigan, Haverford, Connecticut, and Yale, have said in effect that this amounts to taxation without representation, and have refused to pay all or part of their taxes.

In such ways the question of the war comes to the doorstep of the potential draftee, the professor, the Negro, the radical, and the ordinary tax-paying citizen.

One way of articulating the problem is as a dialogue between conscience and law. President Woodrow Wilson in World War I provided a classic illustration of what happens when the first is simply subsumed in the latter. After asking Americans to be neutral in thought as well as deed, after proclaiming that a victor's peace would rest on shifting sands and that what the world must have was "peace without victory," President Wilson later called the war a crusade for democracy, resurrected the posture of unconditional surrender, and hounded out of existence Wobblies, socialists, pacifists, and others less agile than he in reversing the official line. There is an inherent conflict between statesmen, conventionally authorized executioners, and those who, following Camus, insist on striving to become neither executioners nor victims.

But we think it is a fundamental error to portray the problem of civil liberties in wartime as merely a problem of individual conscience. The other side of the question is that in time of war and Cold War the state is out of control. If the rising moon or a wayward flight of geese is interpreted on the radar screen of the early warning network as ICBM's, the President has the apparent power to incinerate us all. We object to any human being having the power to decree the death of millions of others. There is a problem of democracy involved in the enormous present powers of the quasi-mobilized nation-state which must not be shirked by addressing it as a problem of individual freedom only.

Freedom of travel can be defended as a right of conscience,

protected by the First Amendment. But we should like to pose the issue of freedom of travel in a more public context. We want to suggest that whether or not actions such as taking an airplane to Hanoi or sitting-in at a draft board can be considered "speech" under the First Amendment, such actions are necessary to protect man's natural right to life.

But the reader may protest: going to Hanoi or sitting-in at the draft board is against the law, or more precisely, against the law as presently defined. We reply that deliberate law-breaking through nonviolent civil disobedience is a valid, and should become a routine, form of democratic dialogue.

Accepted constitutional doctrine in the United States represents an invitation to hypocrisy. On the one hand it says: think and express yourself freely without consciousness of social obligation. But on the other hand it affirms: do not act on what you believe unless the majority agrees with you, that is, sanctions such action by law. The problem is not merely a personal one. Law itself has grown when individuals defied it. When John Lilburne was hailed before the Star Chamber on the eve of the English Civil War, he refused to answer questions which might incriminate him, saying that he believed his refusal justified by the law of England and knew it to be justified by the law of God. Thus it became part of the law of England. When the Dred Scott decision of 1857 gave Supreme Court approval to the Fugitive Slave Act of 1850, abolitionists defied the assertion of this highest constitutional authority that Negroes could not be American citizens, and deliberately broke the law. In less than ten years, the Fourteenth Amendment made their lawlessness into law. If in historical retrospect one finds such actions good, as we suspect most of our readers would, how can one categorically condemn similar lawbreakers today?

The reader may question if we are justifying the lawbreaking of persons with whom we agree while condemning the lawbreaking of, say, a Southern segregationist. No. If there is a Southern segregationist who is prepared nonviolently to disobey the legislation of recent years and go to jail for it, we support his action on the ground that he may have something to point out to us about those laws which we have not yet seen. The difference between nonviolent civil disobedience and other lawbreaking is that the nonviolent civil disobeyer does not, at least as an immediate consequence, injure anyone but himself.

Yet the reader may ask if the ultimate consequence of this action is not to weaken the law, to weaken the fabric of conventions which keeps us sinful men this side of anarchy. Gandhi and Martin Luther King reply that by accepting punishment the nonviolent civil disobeyer sustains the letter of the law, and by breaking individual laws for conscience's sake the disobeyer keeps alive the spirit of justice on which law ultimately depends. Were it the case that all defiance of law was illegitimate, the right of revolution would also stand condemned and both the Declaration of Independence and Lincoln's First Inaugural Address would have to be discarded. Prudence indeed will dictate that just as peoples are more disposed to suffer than revolt, so one-man revolution also will not be undertaken for light and transient causes. Few men are prepared to court jail terms for the sake of an idea; those who are willing deserve our thanks.

For if, to paraphrase Lincoln, one takes one's stand with the Declaration of Independence, statutory law will be seen as the declarer not the creator of rights, and the law written in the hearts of men will be viewed as the standard by which laws written on paper must be judged. The law of a given conventional jurisdiction will have validity insofar as it enforces the rights of all men. Mankind as a whole, in a nuclear age, will

confront all nation-states as chronic criminals far more dangerous to the rights of man than the solitary nonviolent disobeyer.
By saying No, that disobeyer will seek to recall authority to
common sense.

III

To achieve such international consciousness is the primary task
before all of us Americans. How can Americans feel the way
these Vietnamese do? Put simply, we must understand those
born in a revolutionary condition though we were not. It is a
most difficult task.

Most Americans have no comprehension of rural poverty, of
jungle warfare, of distant Asia. Most Americans know nothing
of revolution. This is most deeply true for the white American
majority, but true in many ways for Negro Americans too.
Many, though not all, American Negroes view the N.L.F. in
the same way that Southern sheriffs view SNCC.

What, then, can we draw upon to understand revolution? Is
it possible for the American majority to think in new ways,
when that majority has slaughtered the Indians and educated
succeeding generations to love General Custer? when that
majority turned black people into property, sold them, tortured and killed them, and for one hundred years after the
Civil War refused to grant them equal rights? when that
majority has experienced victory in each of seven wars our
country has fought, and never felt the rain of bombs falling on
its soil and cities? when that majority feels unsafe at the
slightest threat to its worldwide empire of property, military
bases, and subservient governments?

We can begin to learn about revolution by studying our
own history. As Senator J. W. Fulbright pointed out to Gen-

eral Maxwell Taylor during his committee's 1966 hearings, the American Revolution was a "war of national liberation." The British Army of that time was technically superior to the ragged Americans, but could not coax the patriots out of the trees to fight positional warfare. The Americans received direct support from the French: Senator Frank Church commented during the hearings to Secretary Rusk that "there were as many Frenchmen at Yorktown when Cornwallis surrendered as there were American Continentals." Many British collaborators fled the country to Canada, but no American sheds a tear for them today. The leader of the Revolution, George Washington, was never opposed for the Presidency, but few today would argue that revolutionary America was a totalitarian state. Americans at one time knew what revolution was.

We should know what a civil war is, too. Vietnam contains approximately the same population, thirty million, as the United States at the time of our Civil War. The estimated number of men killed during the Vietminh war was between six hundred thousand and seven hundred thousand, as many as in 1861–65. Try to imagine that after the American Civil War, the oppression of dark-skinned laborers in the South had touched off a new civil war more violent and bloody than the first. Imagine, too, that a foreign nation intervened to put down the rebellion. This is the situation in Vietnam today, and we Americans are the foreign intervenors.

What we additionally need to consider about our Revolution and Civil War, however, is their failure. The Revolution ended with black Americans enslaved. The Civil War and Reconstruction left Southern Negroes voteless, landless, and forgotten. A century later they and other colored minorities still are on the bottom rung of the economic ladder, still doing the work that no white person would be willing to do.

Our country has been significantly imperialist, ethnocentric, indifferent to the cultural riches and human worth of dark-skinned people, from its beginnings.

IV

So history is not enough. Freedom of travel to all countries and for all kinds of persons—poor people as well as professors, SNCC organizers as well as newsmen—is a resource America needs if it is to have any kind of empathy with the experience of most of mankind. It needs freedom of travel to help it make a new start.

When the travelers return they can make contact with their American audiences by drawing an analogy between the lives they encountered in Accra, Havana, or Hanoi and the lives of the rebellious poor of the United States.

American racism already supposes a likeness between SNCC and the Vietcong; and one U.S. public affairs officer has written that "the problem that confronted the government forces in areas penetrated by the V.C. might be compared with the police problem in the slum district of a large American city, say, some parts of Harlem."[4] We, too, must convey the relatedness of these problems, but from the view of the colonized and excluded.

But it is not simply the poor who are excluded from our American empire, though their exclusion is the most severe. What place in the empire is there for the student who wants to question the Cold War or participate in the running of his university? What place in the empire is there for the doctor

---

[4] John Mecklin, *Mission in Torment* (Garden City, N.Y., 1965), p. 82.

who wants to treat those who need treatment most, for the lawyer who wants to represent those who have no representatives? What place for the humanist, liberal or conservative, who wants men to live and let live, who wants Western religions to help the poor of the earth? What place is there for those who cannot find integrity in work, meaning in personal relations, a purpose worth supporting, those who are hounded, despised, feared, examined, cross-examined and sent to institutions?

Together, people such as these could oppose the empire with a community, making an affirmation something like this: We are not responsible for the Cold War. We did not make it. Those are not our plants in Johannesburg, Rio, and Saigon. We own no shares in Engelhard Industries, Kennecott Copper, Lockheed, United Fruit. We have no seats at the Stock Exchange. We did not select George Meany to represent the working people of this country. We are not using classrooms and foundation grants to reinforce the major assumptions of our society. We are not consultants to our President. Not at all. We did not kill Nguyen Van Troi; we did not kill Ben Barka; we did not kill Chaney, Schwerner, and Goodman. We are not at war with the people of Laos, Cambodia, Thailand, and we are not at war with the people of Vietnam. We are not planning and will not support the war which threatens with China.

We are part of the same great family on earth as those Cubans, Ghanaians, and Vietnamese who are trying to make a way independent of the Great Powers, trying to assume the responsibility for decisions which have been expropriated by others, trying to take back the stolen natural resources, the factories, the farming land, the schools, and above all the labor which has been used by others for so long. Those others have had their turn. But their turn is ending, and they will not pass on to us their portfolios, their plantations and mines, their nuclear buttons, and their cattle prods. We will share this earth with all who own it because they live and work on it. In the neighborhoods where we live and work, we must find our own way to be international men.

ABOUT THE AUTHORS

Staughton Lynd is a professor of history at Yale University. Born in Philadelphia in 1929, he is the son of Robert S. and Helen M. Lynd who together wrote *Middletown* and *Middletown in Transition*, the noted sociological studies of Muncie, Indiana. A Quaker, Professor Lynd lives with his wife and children in New Haven, Connecticut.

Thomas Hayden was one of the framers of the Port Huron Statement, the first major position paper of the Students for a Democratic Society. At present he is an organizer with a community union in a Negro section of Newark, New Jersey.